Sue is married and has a son, a daughter and a Scottie dog called George. She has lived in Northumberland for over fifteen years.

After decades of not writing much more than a postcard, angel guidance inspired Sue to pick up the pen…

The results you see in this book represent a year of daily writings. It is a melting pot of emotions, to share, so that others may recognise that we walk the same path, maybe to reach out to a heart that has lost touch… It is a healing which began Sue's own spiritual journey.

After many years working as a school nurse/house mother, and in other 'care' situations, writing became a natural outlet for self-expression on her spiritual path.

God's Beautiful Words

Sue Welfar-Staden

God's Beautiful Words

Sue Welfar-Staden

God's Beautiful Words.
Copyright © 2021 by Sue Welfar-Staden.

All rights reserved. No part of this book may be reproduced in any form or by any electronic or mechanical means, including information storage and retrieval systems, without permission in writing from the publisher and author, except by reviewers, who may quote brief passages in a review.

This publication contains the opinions and ideas of its author. It is intended to provide helpful and informative material on the subjects addressed in the publication. The authors and publisher specifically disclaim all responsibility for any liability, loss, or risk, personal or otherwise, which is incurred as a consequence, directly or indirectly, of the use and application of any of the contents of this book.

Certain stock imagery © Shutterstock.com.

ISBN: 978-1-63950-115-1   [Paperback Edition]
         978-1-63950-116-8   [eBook Edition]

Printed and bound in The United States of America.

Gateway Towards Success

1309 Coffeen Avenue
STE 1200, Sheridan,
Wyoming, 82801 USA
 +13179780258
www.writersapex.com

*This book is dedicated to my husband, Jack.
I thank him for his wisdom and love.*

*I would also like to thank
Pauline Myhill and Alan, her 'angel guide'.*

*Many thanks, also, to Mayya Tukara at www.amissionoflove.org,
who designed the cover for this book and created a similar
design for my website.*

For Beautiful Words and Personal Messages

Visit the Website of Sue Welfar-Staden

www.pureandoriginal.co.uk
and click on the rose…

Preface

A few years ago, I received 'angel guidance' to begin writing. And as the millennium year was fast approaching, I made a commitment that I would write daily. And in truth, I could not bring a conclusion to the day without completing a 'writing' of some description! I knew from the very first that the work was different and the quality set it apart from anything previously written. Each piece revealed a beautiful and pertinent message. And I continue to be moved, by words 'given'. I never fail to respond with wonder, yet I am also still deeply humbled.

Even though the 'messages' were for me – for it was, in actual fact, my 'supported journey' throughout the year 2000 – I have to acknowledge that there was always the desire to share, and more than once that fact was made abundantly clear. A wisdom from somewhere, I felt sure it was a sign that 'Love – Creator – God' is with us now, and speaks to those who would hear His voice in their hearts.

The love of the divine reaches out across the ages. Time and space are no barriers to His message, for it comes over loud and clear. I have no doubt at all that these are 'channelled' words, from an 'intelligence and love' that knows no end. They are given as a light in the hour of need, comfort in sorrow, and for an acknowledgement of joy.

Share with me, in thanks for this miraculous experience called *life*.

Thank you.

1 January

My presence is in your life.

A gift beyond price is yours, to treasure
and to use. Not to put on the shelf and look at now
and then, but to work with awareness, in your
daily existence.

My Love in your soul, to share and let others
see the Light, so that they might
come to know Me.

2 January

There is only one way to live and that
is with Love. A Love for life, which will
permeate all things...

A Love which has no boundaries.
A Love which is incomprehensible and yet
so simple.
This is the gift of which I speak.
To understand, to feel compassion, to share
all that which is yours. To live without fear!

3 January

There are no words other than mine
that will heal and help those who are in pain.
There is no path, other than mine.
It is the only way.

Hear the words, see the bright signs!
Feel the Love that is here! Open your heart,
let peace come in and radiate that joy,
for this is how it was meant to be.
Look to the Light and follow your star.

4 January

My heart hears your cry.
I say again, turn to Me. Turn away
from your sorrow-making activities.

There is not one who cannot be
healed and made whole. Come and
join that throng.

Let your lives be full of My joy; let false
pride and ego be things of the past. The only
way forward is the way of peace.

5 January

I walk with you, for you are My child.
What Loving Father/Mother would
desert their Beloved One?

Yet you become busy and forget Me;
you become all that is not fair and lovely.

One thought of Me, one step with Me,
is sufficient. Take hold of My hand and
I will guide you. Each step shall be joyful,
each step, an adventure into life!

6 January

I seek the careworn, the saddened
and those whose hearts are homeless. I seek
them to let them know that they are not
forgotten. For inside each and everyone
is a part of Me.

Turn again, I say, and let yourselves be
warmed in the glow of My Love, of My
simple peace.
Look therefore and find Me, in the quiet,
in the stillness, in the silence: I am there!

7 January

As I speak to one, so it is for all.
The message stands unchanged. I am
with you in many ways, yet you choose
not to hear. I come in many forms, yet
you choose not to see. I come in many
guises to shake you, for still you are asleep!

There are many diversions,
but ultimately one true path will reach
Me, for I am your destination.
I Light the way.
Stir now and travel that road, sure in the
knowledge that you journey not alone.

8 January

See all with Love and compassion,
for there is nothing that will heal
and comfort, such as these.

See the world in simple terms, for all
was meant to be straightforward.
Complications are mischief's intent
to prevent a good outcome.

See all with Love and understanding,
knowing that all are One.

9 January

You are protected, cradled, in the hands
of Love. Like a small babe, your needs and
wants are provided, without question.

Yet still you turn your hearts away from the Light.
Still, you live your lives in darkness.

Make the decision now, and turn, as a
flower naturally turns its face to the sun
to grow: re-turn to Me.

Seek warmth, seek growth, seek Light!

10 January

Look to your fellow travellers on life's road.
All hit rocky patches;
no one escapes the clutches of despair.

Do not turn away from those who suffer.
Be the friend who knocks upon the door.

Be the one who hears the cry.
Be the one who reaches out
with a Loving heart.

Be the one who is *there*.

11 January

All is working its way through
the intricately woven web of
human experience.

You choose your path, your strand!
It is for your learning.

However far you are away from the shore,
however deep into the wilderness
you stray, one thought only to hold in
your heart: I am at your side.

12 January

Every day is a journey of delight, as
you bathe in My Love, My serenity.

Leave all to Me. Walk with Me, and be
at peace. Know that the power of good
is infinitely stronger than any ill
you could ever imagine.

Stand firm in that understanding,
no matter what may befall.

13 January

Perfect, just as I am...

and in My image made. In Love only
take a day journey into life; trying to
see too far ahead will unnerve.

You were not made to carry the weight
of the unseen future. That is Mine to hold.

Yours is to be all that you can be – today!

14 January

I call you to open your minds.

In simple ways, in many ways, hear
My voice.

For I am there, in the beauty of nature,
in a child's laughter, and in the heart-rending cry
of those who have suffered.

Hear and respond with wonder and delight.
Hear with compassion.

15 January

Take from Me all that is sustaining,
for the well will never run dry.

Take into your hearts the understanding
of My words.

Let go of all that which is not pure, until
your lives radiate My Love.

16 January

Countless say they do not know Me.
For countless do not feel Me in their
lives.

But in truth, I am there. It is a matter
of choice, a matter of perception.

The time is coming, when you will
hear Me, see Me, know Me!

17 January

Let no one be deceived, there are no shadows in which to hide.

For I know all that is, and all that has been...

All thoughts, all deeds, all hearts!

Therefore, hear and be a channel for My Love only, and live in the Light.

18 January

Forgiveness is the start of the healing process – of yourself, when you can accept, you have been wrong or unkind with others.

And forgiveness of those who have hurt you, knowingly or unknowingly,
along the way.

Let forgiveness begin now, and then let it go.
To carry all that you know you are responsible for is too heavy a burden!

19 January

It is never too early in the day, or too
late into the night, to call upon Me.
No matter when or where, call upon Me.

Limit not that which is limitless. Try
not to understand that which is infinite –

and therefore cannot be understood by
the human mind, which tries to confine.

20 January

Being away from Me is like walking
in darkness. Being away from Me
is being alone and friendless.
That should not be. For no one need
be separate.

Draw back the curtain and see Me.
Allow the mists to clear, and see Me.
Let the dawn break!

The awakening comes, for some,
in delicate colours, gently, quietly and
slowly. For many, it is as a bright sun
of illumination!

21 January

There is always an answer, but answers must not consciously be looked for.

For even 'perceived' endings can alter, because of free will.

Ultimately, all will come to know God... to know that all are one, and move on.

22 January

Be still and in silence, see Me.

Be still and hear My words. They are for comfort, for guidance, for joy.

Many things are sent to block your path.

To steer a straight course is not an easy task. Return to Me each time; this is the work that I ask of you.

23 January

All around are My gifts, as yet untapped.
All around is My presence, radiating Light.

Open your heart to feel. For when you cross the threshold, into that knowledge, there can be no end.

It is like coming home, to the One who has loved you for ever. To the One who waited, while you ran off and loved others. Who through your laughter and torments, has waited for tears to clear.

Look up now and know that I was there... all along!

24 January

I have chosen well.

The rock is sure and will not crumble. Long has been the building, and the results are beautiful.

Not one hair of the head will be harmed, for in My protection you now dwell. In acknowledgement of My unconditional Love for you, live your life.

All is well, all shall be well!

25 January

Every breath drawn to sustain life
is given by Me.

Every step taken is watched over by Me.

Therefore have no fear, for all is in order;
all is in place.

The day will come when more will
look to Me, more will walk in My Light.
A day of miracles is approaching.

26 January

Seeking the truth are many hearts
that are heavy;
many who are in despair.

But to be in that place of discomfort
and *recognise*, is the first step.
For even in that place, there is choice.

There is no one who does not know
Me, no one who does not know My name.
Call it from that place, and I will hear.

27 January

Only a great Love can sustain
during the pressures and trials of
earthly life.

Mine alone is that Love – for those
who are aware, for those who seek.

28 January

In My presence, allow yourself to Be.
Give to yourself the gift of silence;
My words will surely come.

This connection is of the Highest.
All solace, peace and Love will be ever present.

To those who knock, the door will be
opened.

29 January

Always on the *outer* side there is turmoil.
For it is the business of Life. Make it
your business to be calm on the *inner* side.
This will produce results not dreamt
of before.

From this peaceful centre will come all
you will ever need to know, all you could
ever hope to bring into your life.

The benefits are limitless. For it is being
in touch with the infinite.

30 January

I am ever watchful. There is not one
I do not know. Unconditional is the
Love that I have for every soul.

When each becomes aware, this will
permeate all aspects of life.

Think of My Love as the radiant light
of the sun, which sustains all life;
for it warms, enhances and brings joy!

31 January

At all times, know that I am present.
Only the hardening of your hearts
makes this difficult to believe.

Look for Me, face Me and you will know
such joy!
So many gifts I have bestowed; but in
greed they have been defiled.

Turn again, to know Me and rediscover
your true self.

1 February

Let your grief fade.

For all those you Love are with Me.
Let your remembrance only be of the
joy that's known.

Sadness and joy are as one. It is
the personality which feels the emotion.
The soul, when it returns to source,
knows only great peace, with
unconditional and continuous Love.

You can experience a drop of that
ocean now, by coming to Me in your
awareness. I hold a place in readiness
for your return.

2 February

Come to Me! Lay down all that can
cause concern. Bring to Me your heavy
burdens, for My arm is strong and can
carry all.

Do not question how. Accept, with a
child's trust and simplicity. Accept,
just as you accept the air to breathe.

For in the palm of My hand you are safely
held. In your joy and in your suffering,
know that you are enfolded in My Love,
My truth!

3 February

Hear the tender words.
Know that there are no reproaches
for past disbelief – only rejoicing, that you
have opened your ears, eyes and heart.

A great Love awaits those who allow
themselves to respond. Know that I walk
with you. Stand with courage, against
all adversity, in the Light of My Love.

4 February

Beautiful are the moments when in
stillness you connect with Light. Great
is the peace, and unsurpassed the joy.

This is My gift to you who walk this path,
for it is not a smooth terrain. There will
be times of solitude, of struggle,
torment and indecision.

Balance and strength will come,
when you take time to be with Me.

5 February

Call on Me, when you are in trouble,
or when you have lost your way. For I am
your guide and your direction finder.

Call on Me, to Light your path.
All that you ever need is within My power
to grant; yours is to ask.

6 February

Do not revisit past, painful memories.
To do so brings them into your
present, and thus your future.

Decide to forgive all that holds them
within you. Forgive and move on, for
it takes energy.

Use that gift of life's vitality, to live and
speak only with Love. Let go of all that
has wounded, and begin each day anew...
with Me!

7 February

At one with Me. No higher can be reached! How beautiful the words, *At one with Me.*

Give up the trying to work it out. Or the trying to sort it out, for it is in My hands. All the drama and turmoil of life is for learning.

When you can be at peace within your heart, in the midst of all storms and confusions, you will have found My peace, and be *at one with Me.*

8 February

Dark are the forces that gather, to blow
you off course. Strong are the emotions,
that would ensnare and drag you down.

Fight all, with My name, My Love,
My courage!
There is no other way, for it is the eternal
battle of life – of negative and positive.
With My help, restore peace, restore balance.

9 February

Nature – My perfection, My beauty!
Are My gifts to you not freely given?
These places can be mirrored within
your heart.

For these are days of confusion,
uncertainty, competition and fear.
Make time for awareness of the peace
within nature: it is there.

I am that peace which you seek!

10 February

You still think you can do it on your own;
you cannot. For you were never
meant to; but if you were to turn just
a little, you would see Me at your side.

Know that I am with you, and you do
not have to face even your smallest fear
alone. Believe it and know it is true!
I would not say otherwise; why do you
doubt so? You close your ears, and your heart
remains hard. Soften, and allow Me
to enter your life.

11 February

Make each day a fresh start, a new beginning. Let the old day fade, and along with it all sorrow and misfortune.

To carry any burden is to amass a weight. You were not fashioned so. Take with you only thoughts of the joyous.

Be together in My name.
For strong indeed are such unions. Those who live in My Love cannot be divided. Invincible are two minds and souls with but one heart. Infuse your lives with My peace, for the outer world can never be your true friend: I am.

12 February

Come to me. Tell me your heart's concerns, share with Me your daily lives.

Do not make Me a stranger. For I stand before you, in precious Love, waiting to be called. I am your friend at the gate, waiting to be asked in.

But you have built up walls so strong, almost impenetrable at times. Do not wait until death or destruction loom. Open the way to your heart and speak with Me, now!

13 February

Live your life as a prayer of thanksgiving
for all the wondrous gifts freely given.
Gifts given that require payment
demand a different response.

Love which is given without condition
can only be met with incredulity.
Send out only thoughts of Love, feelings
of joy; these alone will create positivity.
Connect with Light in the airwaves,
and instantaneous will be awareness
throughout all eternity!

14 February

All have their own work to do; you
cannot do it for another. You may, in Love,
support and guide.

It is only when another chooses
to hear, that a shift may be made.
Do not cajole, for no one can know what
experience has been chosen;
it is not yours to know.

The greatest work is to stand back; be
only a reflection of the Light. Be your
true self, and in being so, another may
see you and respond.

15 February

Do you not know, My angels watch over your every move? Let the joy of that awareness overspill to others.

Yours to see, yours to acknowledge – for if you look, they will be there. This is My gift to you; it is a blessing.

In all your difficulties, all your trials, remember this; you are surrounded by Light. Your daily prayers will strengthen this connection!

16 February

No one knows the hour of My coming;
for it will be different for all, as each
one responds, in turn, to My Words!

Come back to Me, in your hearts,
and know that in the hands of Love
you are safely held.

Come back to Me, and there will be no
need for further search or journey! To
the eternal question of life, I am the
only answer.

17 February

Be still, and behold My glory. For in
this moment, you are truly with Me.

Know that this is a time of rediscovery,
of rest and of regrouping. There is
so much to learn.

Experiences and challenges are sent to
shake you up. Hold only Light within
your being.

18 February

Let Me be your life force within. Close your eyes and ears to the clamour of the outer world. For connection with Me is beyond comprehension.

When you absorb My Love into your being, you will radiate peace, energy, strength and knowledge.

19 February

Spend time in nature, and allow your mind to grasp the concept of *oneness*.

Connect with the Divine continuous circle of creation – the giving and receiving, the sustaining of all life.

The returning of the physical to earth and atmosphere is My perfection.

20 February

From the dawn of time, I have been with you, as your soul journeyed. I guide you now, as always with directive nudges, to encourage.

Humanity has free will; therefore, all are responsible. All exists 'now'; be still and absorb, for all are on a return pathway to the source. To know this is to be there.

21 February

My words, your work, will allow others to know that they, too, can go beyond their existing confines.

To align with your faith will inspire many to dare, to be brave!

To know too that their birthright is to reach beyond the stars and touch with the Infinite.

22 February

In a crowded place, My children shine forth like pinpoints of Light.

They will attract, for one will recognise another.

There can be no hiding, and wherever they meet together, the quality will be immeasurable.

23 February

There is no need for outward show or gesture. Gently, quietly, go about My work.

Each day, light a candle for purity and remembrance. It will also attract more Light! Know that I am with you. In My presence, be still and be aware that My angels encircle you.

Let all know that it is so!

24 February

You called to Me in anguish, and I heard. For there is not one who is turned away.

Every day, a healing is breathed into your being. Most precious is the time spent in quietness, with Me.

For in those moments, awareness and insights are imparted. Let the 'little' self move aside, connect with the universal truth and know that you are travelling through.

25 February

When you find Me and walk this road, know that it has to be one of determination and sacrifice.

For never again will you live as before. It will be a giving up of all that you once were. To be born anew, in Me; to become all that you can be.

Fuse with Me now, and know there is no other way. Countless souls search for peace... Stay in silence and absorb all that I offer.

26 February

All that you hold close to yourself, and all
that you hold in high esteem, will not, in
days of trouble, protect or surround you
with Love.
For I am all that you need.

When I am within and without, all of
this world becomes as nought.
For you now follow a Light which burns
more brightly and will not be denied.

27 February

Look to the bright stars shining, and
when all seems lost, they will remind
you that I am with you, in all.
You cannot separate joy from sadness,
for it is the way of life.

Things happen in equal number, but
your nature remembers only too well
the sadness. Joyful moments are taken
as granted. It is a matter of balance.

I know your heart: come to Me, devoid
of pretence.

28 February

You have slept enough!

Wake now, and be with Me, in your awareness. Hear Me, wake now and do My work.

I give all for you; give now a little of yourself, in return.

29 February

I wait patiently for you to call upon Me.
I wait for you to recognise that there
can be one way, one eventual conclusion.

And that is to bring Me back into your
life. It is so simple! Humanity cries for Love;
I am that Love! I am the flame whose Light
will never be extinguished.

1 March

Still you seek comfort and peace,
in the desert place.
There are none that can do so.
For nourishment cannot be found in the
arid wastelands.

You have forgotten who you are:
you are My children. And I call you home,
to the oasis, to the well.
For only in Me will you find
that for which you search.

2 March

Seek the company of the enlightened.
For their wisdom and compassion
will enhance your endeavours.

There will be many who would take your
energy and Love, without you knowing,
and without care for you.

Guard yourself from those who would
drain your life force.

3 March

Know indeed that I walk beside you,
as you carry your burdens. Look now
and see Me.

Know that I am there, not to take your
life lessons completely, but to share.
For the work that you are doing is for
Me. Your perseverance and Love for Me
shines through every moment, in every day.

Walk this path unfalteringly and rejoicing,
for it is an acknowledgement.
Love nailed to the cross is redeemed,
and lives in the hearts of all those who recognise.

4 March

I am beyond all imagination.
Even the most generous of human hearts
and minds cannot find the words.

I am beyond all concept. I am Love –
beyond all knowledge!

One step towards Me will be sufficient
to feel the magnificence and beauty of
My gentle peace.
Take that step!

5 March

There is great joy awaiting all those
who respond to My words.

For the world's noises try to deafen
and distract.

Commitment and dedication must be
the aim of all those who wish to
know Me, and find a better way –
the only way!

6 March

It is possible to achieve a state of oneness through regular prayer and meditation.

Choose a way of being, rather than allowing life to just happen.

No matter where, when, or why you seek, you will find Me!

7 March

You are all firmly entrenched in 'what or who' you think you are. The truth is that you are far more than you can ever imagine.

The exterior is a harbour, a place for the spirit to dwell whilst on this earthly journey.

If you desire understanding and wisdom, you must look! Teachers will appear in many guises. Openness and intelligence will alert you to their presence.

8 March

Know that I am with you as you travel. No matter where you go, I am with you!

This is so for all, whether or not they are aware.

So rest gently now in this knowledge, and let it be your strength!

9 March

Always guided, always protected. For you are My precious children – so beautiful, so pure!

May your courage allow you to stand in My name, and take you along life's highway.

Many fall by the wayside, and cry for an easy task. But what is it that I ask of you?

Only that you look to Me, and live your faith.

10 March

Be like one who never fails to make time
to rejoice in My name.

A habit of closeness with Me, once cultivated,
will help create Light, Love and trust,
in days of distress.

Closeness with Me will enable Light to
penetrate even the most dense darkness.

Make time now to be with Me, your friend.

11 March

Every soul will return to source, for it is
the Creator's plan.

All have eternity in which to experience.
Free will allows each to decide their path.

All must learn that Love alone is the
answer, to any question, any situation!

12 March

I choose My workers, for there are
qualities in them. They are beyond
reproach, and My Love is in their lives.

They reflect My glory from their hearts,
and others will recognise My truth in them.
There are many who still make mockery,
but they will come to know that I am
there, in all of life.

I am the beginning and the end. This is
the truth – theirs to learn,
in a flash of inspiration,
or gentle blossoming of awareness.

13 March

Each can only start from where they
now stand.
No one can push or cajole another; it is
solely the choice of the individual

whether to seek Me, and move towards
understanding, or to remain entrenched
in earthly matters.

14 March

From the beginning of time, I am.
Unto the end of all worlds, I am.
All in between comes into being
only through My Love.

I give mankind the gift of free will, to
learn that the universe is outstanding –
unparalleled in Love and intelligence.

That alone is the truth, which will overcome
all evil.

15 March

Continually with Me now, and throughout
all eternity.

In My Love connected, at one with
all things, all of life.

One thought joins all, separation ceases.

16 March

My ways are the ways of honesty, integrity, justice, compassion and forgiveness. Having a Love for humanity as it exists now...

a Love which is non-judgmental and overflowing!

When you are at peace with Me, these will be your ways.

17 March

I send angels of beauty, of grace, of healing. They are on the earth-plane at all times, in all places.

They watch and see where they can assist mankind. But it may not be until after an encounter that you might wonder...

18 March

I will speak to you now, with clarity.

Yours will be to help others who have lost their way and who are in despair.

Let them know that they can find all they need – in Me!

19 March

Do not be afraid to speak of Me, to profess My name for ever.

Those who ridicule and live ungodly lives will call upon Me, in the hour of their greatest need.

They will come to know My Love through your words, your actions.

20 March

And He said to them, 'Fear not.'
I say this again to you now: 'Fear not!'
For nothing can harm you. Pray daily
in My name.

Ask for all the blessings that are so
rightfully yours. Ask, as a child would
ask of his Loving Father!

21 March

Let those who have departed from this
life move on.
Do not allow your fears or sadness hold
their spirits back. They are now free
from earthly concerns.

No matter in what way they passed over,
they rest in a state of bliss, or are moving
towards it...
Let your thoughts only be of Love shared
For in an instant, they can be with you,
by thought alone.

Time and space cannot separate.

22 March

Enter into My house with a pure heart,
for all is known by Me.

Know that My way for you is already
planned.

You will be guided in dreams, visions and
moments of insight.
Take each in joy and gratitude,
and multiplied will be all your blessings!

23 March

All one now, and throughout all
eternity. Grasp this intelligence;
it is fundamental to realisation.

The cycle of life, never ending.
All returning, until all stand in the
presence of the Divine.
For it is indeed a spiritual journey.

24 March

You can count on Me; can I count on you? Will you stand firm in My Name?

Will you always make time each day, to bide in silence?

For these times will allow you to hear My words. There is so much that it will undoubtedly bring many others who will want to know Me!

25 March

Let My Love touch your heart, let My Love hold you for ever.

For I am that part of you which will never die, and your soul-spirit is a part of Me.
In this we are one, unchanging, never ceasing.

26 March

Look into the eyes of the One who died
upon the cross, and still say, 'I do not know.'
You will not, for you cannot.

For you will see a pure Love –
a Love beyond comprehension; a Love
that has a deep knowledge of your very
soul.

Look into the eyes, and you will recognise
the One who has always known you.

27 March

Only the courageous are given tasks
beyond the capabilities of the 'normal' person.
Those who would endure the struggle
of earthly confusions are given the
strength to bear.

These are the doers, the torch bearers,
the pathfinders. You may not know it
at this moment, but My Light pours on
you, through you and around you!
Then it can only radiate out from you,
to touch many.

28 March

Do not let troublesome thoughts
pervade and disturb; think only of
My Love for you.

Come into My calm, come into My
peace, and from that centre, which
knows only bliss, live your life.

29 March

Look forward to your time spent with
Me. For I am the honoured guest who calls.

I am the One whom you wait to receive.
There are no times more beautifully spent
than these. For it is this that will inspire
you to go on to be of help to others. All
fears will melt away.

30 March

Know that your lives are touched by
the hand of an intelligence that knows
no barriers.

Touched by a Divine Love which
transcends time and distance,
touched by a joy, it is infinite.

Leave your calculating thoughts behind,
open your heart and know this truth.

31 March

Connect with Love, and know that I
am there.
Connect with Light, and know that I
am in your life.

Let My presence transcend all. For
when you walk with Me, you will
not want to be as before.

See all as challenges; never think of
failure, for there are no mistakes.
The very striving to be with Me will
take you there.

1 April

I have chosen you for My work.

For I see a pure soul, and one who will
be Mine. For has this not always been so?

We have walked together, a little distant
at times...

But when you were ready to hear, I was there.

2 April

Past, present and future are known to Me.
There is nothing hidden from My
sight. In times of need, I call upon the
Faithful Ones, who carry out My work
unflinchingly.

They are the pure, in mind, heart and
spirit. They are of the Light, of goodness,
and they are in such number! All evil will
be overcome, for none can stand against the
power of the Light.

I wait for you to call upon Me, to give you
guidance. I know your path; it can be
illuminated by My wisdom.
Call upon Me now.
Be alert to the signs that are sent.
Trust that I only do what is best for you.

3 April

Nowhere else to go...
nowhere else to be, other than with Me.
Let all rest now, in My name. My desire
is that you relinquish the 'self'
and allow My presence to hold all.
Have faith in God.

4 April

I have known you since time began.
Long have we journeyed together. The
soul dictates its role for the duration,
and throughout each experience, I have
been with you.

When you are ready to hear, allow Me
to come through, in the beauty of
silence.

Allow immeasurable peace to pervade.
Allow a sense of well-being and trust.

5 April

Let yourself see beyond this dark tunnel. For there is indeed a Light that beckons.

That Light encompasses all that I am. I send My angels to look after you.

Do not despair, for you are indeed of the Light, and here to work for Me. Be aware of this.

6 April

Only through great suffering and pain are changes made; therefore do not be unnerved. From the demise of an old way of being comes the birth of the new.

Each moment gives opportunity for rebirth. Make a conscious decision to be reborn in Me.

For only truth, courage and honesty, will suffice. There is no other way to be.

7 April

I am closer than you know, or can ever believe. Closer than life itself. To all who undertake sacrifice in My name, great shall be the rewards.

The long journey, alone and through the dark, is made with Me at your side.

I am closer than you know!

8 April

The gentle hand of Love is your gift to impart. The gentle heart of compassion is yours to share.

Let the Light shine through the gloom and let it become your life, until you become the Light.
Know that all is not lost. For an ending is but a new beginning. Life is but a circle, a spiral, on which all travel.

Have faith in that process, for it applies to each and every one. Only know that the Love, which glues the universe together, is working for you.

Learn to Love and have respect, for the person that you are. Work at being in peace, and you will find your 'self' within that peace.

9 April

Not one teardrop goes unnoticed,
for, when shed in sorrow for Love,
they touch My heart.
Know truly that all cries are heard,
all prayers answered. Ask not only in
the hour of your need, but continually.

For you and I walk together. Nothing can
separate Love of the highest nature – no
matter who gives, or who receives.
Life or death, time or distance, nothing
will or can separate.

10 April

Mine to give, Mine to take, but all is
in order.

Tears may flow, laughter may fill the
air, but all is in My keeping. Do not
delve overmuch, for it is only Mine to
know.

Yours to live. Yours to become aware.
Yours to choose Me!

11 April

I guide your hand, I guide your Life.
And when days are troubled and endless,
think only of Me. Let My sustaining gift
of Love, be all.

There will be no indecision. You know what
you must do, you must do what is right.
I will be with you, as you take that journey.

12 April

I speak constantly with you, but are
you listening?

Your ears and heart are many times
oblivious of My voice. If you choose not
to hear My message, I will turn away...
But when you are ready, I will be here.

For I am eternity!

13 April

Come to Me, not with notions of pride,
but with surrender and humility.

Come to Me, in reverence, acceptance
and joy!

My Love will bathe your soul and soothe
all fears. For the Light that I am
is in your heart. So come to Me.

14 April

Life, and your perception of life, is changing so rapidly. All are here for many reasons; multitudinous are the paths of learning.

Each must come to the only conclusion, and that is to see My Love in all things.

No one can dictate the thoughts of another. By action, intelligence and passion are men inflamed to know Me.

Take the action that would inspire; speak with passion to profess My name, so that others will be stirred. Love Me, as I have Loved you! Be willing to 'die' for Me, as I 'died' for you.

15 April

Not alone, for you walk with Me, and I
with you. Look deep into your heart
and let go of old wounds and hurts.
For those can direct present behaviour.

Focus on inner healing. For it is now time
to put a golden light all around you,
all that you have ever been, or have
experienced, in whatever way.
Let that Light heal all, and be at peace.

16 April

My words are given to raise awareness
of My presence, which is in and around all.
Given as a Light to guide you
every day.

Many things happen, and are sent to
make you question how you have become
entrenched.
Many things happen to shake you
out of the lethargic pattern that you have
allowed to set around your way of being
and thinking. Take notice, keep awake.
Hear my voice in all.

17 April

Focus on Love, focus on its healing
qualities. For all is accomplished by
Love only, all is made whole.
It is a power beyond human intelligence;
but when a few together focus on Love
and Light, miracles occur.

Tender heart, have courage; you are truly
blessed and are surrounded by My Light.
Take all that comes your way as trials, to
be overcome in My name, for My glory. The
Love that you show will lead others to Me.

18 April

In a moment you will realise
what you have been searching for.
Forces that work together for good are
ever present, ever preparing the way.

The journey from the head to the heart
can be long and hazardous.

But in a moment you will know Me, you
will see Me more clearly.

19 April

I watch; I know your trials. Stand firm in your faith, for it is the only answer.

I have chosen you for a special work, encompassing the most fraught of journeys.

You stand alone, but for Me.

20 April

The noblest of all lives are those lived in selfless service.
Those who live as such are nearer to Me than they could ever imagine.

Nothing surpasses recognition of Me and the acknowledgement of My work. Work now to this end. Work, as one, with little time. Work, for Me.

21 April

All is governed by Me. Nothing is left
to chance. All is in place for the soul
to experience.

Many have not grasped this concept,
as widespread spiritual education does not
exist. It must be made known.

Each must hear truth. Each must come
to its realisation and perfection –
a mirror image of Me.
Each must do their own work.

Surrender the ego, give up the pride;
they are not worthy companions.
Love is all!

22 April

It is now a time of tremendous change.
My energies are coming into the world.
My Love infuses those who will respond.

It must be so. For the earth, this precious
cosmic jewel, cannot be left to an
uncertain future in the hands of those whose
only concern is greed. They are unaware of
the possible outcome of their actions.

Those who are awake and hear Me
will work alongside countless thousands.
They will be called the Warriors for Peace.

23 April

Let the knowledge of the risen Lord
be your gateway to understanding.
The joy that surpasses all: He is risen.
Death is no more.

He undertook the supreme sacrifice, in order
to let you know that death is but
a passing and, in Me, you live.
Make each day a day of preparation,
Each moment a step towards your goal.

Remember your purpose.
Focused thought, focused meditation.
Turn your life over to God; He will guide you.
Through vision and insight, He will
be your support.

24 April

As no other shall you be, for you are
My child. My Love now enfolds every
aspect of your being.
It is with such rejoicing that one is
welcomed; it is with such joy.

But this awareness is not without its
struggles; for you now fight a harder battle.

Know that you do not stand alone,
but with the forces of heaven behind you!

25 April

Who makes the *rules*?
Who imposes rules upon you?

None but the self – and an illusion,
created by a child, and how a situation
was perceived. For this is what has
brought you to where you are today.

Look deep within, because a desperate child
controls the adult.
Recognition of this is the first step
to healing, and returning to the true self.

26 April

Each moment is a journey of self-discovery. Each day, a journey homewards.

But only you can take the steps; only you decide your direction.

Remember – balance in all things. Remember that all earthly matters are not sufficient. Turmoil results when you take your way, unaccompanied by Me!

27 April

The way will unfold...
Have courage while all seems uncertain, for many difficulties would overwhelm.

It is a testing time. Hold onto that which you know is right, for all will be revealed. All is in order.

There can be no pushing or straining. As in nature, all develops in its own time, its own way. All results are truly beautiful! Be thankful for all learning.

28 April

Give up all thoughts, save those of Me.
Give up all your commitments, save those to Me.

Decide now, for there can be no half measures.
I am calling you!

Do you see Me? Do you hear Me?

29 April

Come to Me in thanksgiving, come to
Me in joy! For it is the cheerful heart
that I acknowledge. Those who turn to
Me, know Me as their trusted friend.

No matter what the calamity, return to
peace, return to Me. I hear your cry;
it has not gone unnoticed.

Be still, and soon it will be clear,
soon you will know. The shepherd looks for
the one lost sheep. The Father awaits the
return of His beloved son. And when in
sight, rejoicing may begin.
For there is no other that loves and
knows you as I do.

30 April

All are beautiful beings. For My Light shines in each and every one. Be aware of this, and unburden your hearts!

Do not judge anything, for even those hurtling towards possible disaster are learning their lesson.

I am unchanging, in an ever changing world. You are ever searching, ever struggling, always balancing the many facets of human experience.

Time now to accept; time now to allow confusion to disperse. Come into My peace, for I am the only constant in the midst of worldly turmoil.

1 May

My Love is not just for the chosen few,
but for all.

Open your hearts and minds just a little,
and My Light will stream into
all the most deep and dark recesses.

Let it work on these places, that you
have skilfully hidden away for so long.
You have hidden them so well, from all eyes,
including your own...

but not from Mine.

2 May

Angels, in countless numbers, are here.
They are My representatives, and they
do My bidding.

Their duty is to protect and help.
Their work is of the highest, and in My name
they come.

To have a sighting, or knowledge of the
presence of an angel, is indeed a special gift.

3 May

Share all that you have, for all is but a gift –
from Me. And by its passing on,
in Love only, the benefits are multiplied,
the delights increased!

Never hold back a good intention, for it
comes from Me.
I am urging you to acknowledge and trust
that the supply is eternal and abundant.

4 May

Hold a vision for peace, hold a vision
for healing.

The world and its inhabitants
are sorely in need of the power of positive
thought.

5 May

All over the world, the desire for peace
is now at its greatest.
Millions have called, and have been heard.

The Great Ones respond, as in times
past, to the heartfelt cry of humanity.

As all band together to ask for help, they
need only know that their prayers are heard.

6 May

All pure hearts turn naturally to Me.
For they are Mine without question.

All these are on a pathway of Love and Light,
and have a swift passage into My
presence.

But all are My children, no matter what,
and I will never desert them.
How many are the words spoken?
Yet it is only the true heart and generous spirit
for which I ask.

7 May

In all your actions, know that I am
ever present.

Not as one who would intrude, but as
one who Loves you unconditionally.

One who would guide, with wisdom.

8 May

When things do not seem to work out,
walk down another road.

Make a decision to change. That will
take courage, for all get caught up in
old, familiar behaviours.

You think that is all your experience can
ever be, but it is not so.
See the rainbow and the pot of gold,
for they are truly yours to discover.

9 May

The spirit of goodness lies within.
Make a conscious effort to be aware
of that presence.

This knowledge will connect you to
unlimited energy.

Make a decision to merge and become
one with all that is.

10 May

All is change; I am the only constant.
But do not look for Me. Do not seek to
procure that which cannot be contained.

All is change; there does not exist anything
upon this earth which is static. All
emerged from One, and all shall return.

Claim these times as your own, for they are
a blessing, a sacred gift, surpassing all
other, beautiful to behold, and refreshing
to the soul.

11 May

In your wisdom, let go of all that which holds you back and keeps you bound to old ways.

Let go of all that which no longer serves you. Seek only that which enhances and radiates My Love.

12 May

Make a special commitment to come into My presence and be at peace with Me.

All life exists as circles within circles, wheels within wheels. Not one aspect is separate.

All have need of each other and one sustains another. And in all, see Me.

13 May

In the stillness of meditation, you will
connect with your higher self,
and within that process, a universal
intelligence.

Many dismiss this, but know, as you
raise your consciousness, you will walk
upon another pathway.

All that was previously closed and
unresponsive will work in a way
that you would consider miraculous.

14 May

Beautiful words are given, to touch
the heart, to heal the hurt;
to give encouragement and direction
and to be meaningful to all.

For each will interpret according to
their needs, at the time of reading.

Turn and find Me in all things, as well
as beautiful words.

15 May

Help is always at hand, but in your
confusions you do not see.
For the challenge is to be at peace.
When you allow yourself to be taken from your
calm centre, chaos ensues.

Learn to be, therefore, always at peace:
this is the goal for which to strive.

Be in the calm centre, while the storm rages.
Be the calm centre, where the storm cannot reach.

16 May

What is it that you wish to achieve?
Your thoughts are powerful, and can create.
They will bring themselves into reality.

So decide on what to heed. Be
more determined than your wayward thought.
Decide to focus on Love and
compassion; for they are worthy companions,
and will serve you well.

Each day will be meaningful and beautiful.
Each moment, to be savoured.
Each breath, a miracle.
Each heartbeat, a gift that enables...
Bring your awareness and gratitude to bear
on what you consider small; and when studied,
you will realise the enormity, complexity and
wonder of creation.

17 May

And in a moment, you will know Me.
For I have been with you always, I walk
at your side.

But ego and pride struggle continuously
for supremacy while I wait patiently.
For when all else fails, leaving you wounded
and sore, I will be there, with Love, to heal –
and in a moment, you will know Me!

18 May

Powerful, yet gentle; calm, yet exuberant!
Secure, yet free are you in My care.

All is given to nurture. All is given
for contentment. You exist in a heaven
under heaven.

Let your focused thought bring Light
into many lives.

19 May

Be prepared to stand apart. The crowd will not want to share the path that you must tread.

Be prepared to be misunderstood, to be thought odd; for indeed you are.

You travel a different road from most, and there can be no turning back. In the hour of your greatest need, you called upon Me! From that moment, we walk as one.

20 May

The way of true and sincere wisdom, is walked by such a few. Many are entrapped by the snares of a busy world.

And yet it is a dream that is taken for reality. Move on, and see it for what it is.

21 May

True healing can only begin with inner peace; for this alone will result in outer harmony.

All get caught up in the intricacies of life, but there is no need.

Be at peace within, and allow a greater result to manifest.

22 May

Do not turn away from the crying child.

For all are My children. When you respond with Love and the purest of intentions, know that this is recognised!

23 May

Have no fear of imagined future events.
For My Light surrounds and protects you.
All is long predestined, all is sent
for learning.

All is evolving. Many times you stumble,
many times you fall. You call out
in your distress, but it is in the picking up,
the restoration, that you will eventually,
find a better way to be.

In the stillness
My words are given for comfort; they are
wisdom beyond measure. The world calls out
for Love. Look only for peace within,
for that is the basis of Love. And all will be
healed, all will be well!

24 May

Walk gently through the night, for the dawn will come. And with the sun arising comes the promise of a new day!

Walk in the Light, and be not afraid, for I am with you every step of the way. Let My Love for you wash away all cares. As with peaceful, flowing water, you will be cleansed and made whole.

In simple beauty, I am.
In the Love of one for another, I am.

25 May

Cultivate a faith so strong, that nothing will disturb it. Visualise a golden future, not only for those dear to you, but for all.

As you wish to become, be it now; for as you are, so will you attract.

Find in Me the peace that you need.
Find in Me your strength.
In days of confusion, look to Me and know the truth! I am always with you, and My Love will uphold.

26 May

Your trust makes clear My way. Your knowing will help others. In this be sure: I am there in all things, all ways.

Hold My hand, and we will walk together as friends, as companions. Like those who have a deep Love of one for the other.

27 May

This time for you, this time for Me.
Together, in Love, must the work be done.

Great the Love, great the work! For there
is nothing that cannot be achieved.

Seas crossed, mountains climbed.
Every day of your life, you face this,
and more! Rest now in Me, and allow the One
who sees all to guide you.

28 May

Be gentle with others, be gentle with
yourself. No one will be as harsh
as you are to yourself.

Be thoughtful, and allow only wise and
generous words to be spoken. Be silent
on all other matters.

There is no single clear-cut perception.
Remember, all is illusion, all set up to
create learning. Once that is understood,
you become the teacher.

29 May

Be only with Me, in a temple of peace.
Be only with Me, in a garden of beauty.

For there will I give to you a wisdom
beyond your years.

I prepare you for great change. Prepared,
as a child would be for a long journey.

For you would not travel without
guidance, nourishment, nor yet an idea
of your destination.

30 May

Make time, to let the butterfly settle
on your shoulder!

31 May

It is an age of enlightenment, an age
of selfless Love. There is an awareness
of a moving on in thought, word and deed,
as never before.

Let old wounds and ancient scars fade.
Keeping them open and sore revives
the pain anew, which then remains in
your energy.

Love, compassion and forgiveness
lie at the gateway of healing – for yourself
and others.

1 June

Each day is a unique masterpiece in
your life. Each moment, a stitch in
the tapestry.

Let all thoughts of how it should be,
or of how you think others should see you,
disperse.

Act, think and speak only with a
genuine manner, not wishing harm
or hurt to any living creature.

2 June

Hear now words of wisdom. Live as an
example to all, so that they may come
to know the way of truth and sincerity.

Let your heart beat as one with the
universe. It is the dwelling place of
all creation. None can hide their hearts,
or their thoughts.

For that which lies within is seen in the eyes
and heard upon the lips.

3 June

Hour after hour, keep in My company.
Day after day, know Me as your friend.

Long have I known your concerns,
long have I been the One to whom you must
turn. For I am the One who will never
fail you.

Many are unaware of My presence, but I
am there, hour after hour, day after day.

4 June

The work that I ask you to do
will not be easy. You will not take
the well-trodden path.

Most will not want to walk with you;
there will be a few of like mind, but
most will turn away.

The work that I ask you to do will only
be accomplished by complete faith and trust
in Me. There will be little earthly
glory or recognition; it will be a way of
trials – but also of joys!

5 June

Only the highest calls to you. There can be no refusing, for who would turn from God?

Millions who know of Him do so. Millions still do not know of His Love.

The time will come when all will know. Soon, all will acknowledge!

6 June

The spiritual journey cannot be made into a race, for each soul is at its own point of awareness.

All are lost sheep, experiencing separation from the Love of God. Know that His Love never abandoned a single Lamb.

It is awareness of that complete and perfect Love, which returns all to the fold of the Creator.

7 June

With every breath, draw into your
being the perfection of all that I am.

With every beat of your heart, draw in
My Love, which is the answer to all.

A Love which is pure and sincere.
A Love which needs no 'service' in return.

Look deeply, now, into your own heart
and you will know if that Love abides there.

8 June

Trials beset you and cause distress:
give it all up to Me. For there is no
other way that will serve.

Only I have the capacity to see all and
know all. Yours is to trust and give it
all up to Me.

Let there be no other Love in your life
greater than Mine. No way to be,
other than Mine. For My way is of the Divine.
My way encompasses past, present and future
and is only Mine to know.

9 June

I will arise and go to My Father and say,

'I have sinned against you and against Heaven and am no longer worthy to be called your Son.'

Know now that all have been false, and yet all have been true! In My eyes, all are My children, whom I would readily forgive and welcome home.

10 June

Where to go now, for there is nowhere on the outside. The only place to go is within.

Seek to understand who or what you are; seek to know the self.

And in that searching, there must be a fading of the old and an acceptance of the birth of a new refined self.

A self that is at one with all.

11 June

Take My crown, and place it over your head: it will pour blessings upon you.

For those whose hearts are open and pure, whose minds are aware, cannot help but be a part of My Kingdom
and its blessings.

Fear not, for none can harm you, none can destroy your soul.

12 June

And it shall be as I have directed.
No one shall ultimately overcome Me.
My word is law. My word is Love.

This has been made plain to countless generations. How many times, how many ways, must it be spelt out to you? The universe is governed by a set of laws, each complete in its divinity; each one passed down through civilisations. All must be in harmony, all must be in balance, to create well-being.

But this is an age of incredible turmoil, of a clash between dark and light! A clash of all cultures, of old and new ways. Stand firm! Hold onto that which comes from the Light. For only that must succeed. Only that will succeed, to create a promised golden future.

13 June

All are equal in My sight. All are
inheritors of My Love. There is not
one who stands outside the gate.

Although many do not truly understand,
they are encouraged, by Loving guidance,
to follow their soul's path.
For that is the true goal of all
who travel this journey.

14 June

This is a resting time…
a time to regain lost energy, lost focus.

There are many ways of expressing the
self; many ways of becoming who you
are. And who you really are is connected
to the universal energy.

15 June

Let not your heart be troubled – for that emotion is as unreal as its opposite. All are but fleeting shadows.

Cultivate balance, and be aware of the wisdom at the calm centre; for it is there.

Let that voice alone give direction, for it will reveal your true being. That is the moment when I claim My own.

16 June

I give to you a glimpse of what lies
beyond the veil. For you have knocked
and the door has opened; you have
touched Heaven's heart.

Share this glimpse with whoever you can.
For there are many who struggle
in darkness, many who know nothing
of My Love.

There will come a time when all will realise
that there is more to this life
than that which is apparent; far more to man's
existence than he is aware.
Be mindful of Me, keep Me in your life.
For above all, I am mindful of you!

17 June

Take off your shoes, for the ground
upon which you stand is holy ground. All
ground is holy, for it is blessed by Me.

Yet mankind has destroyed and has
allowed corrupt dealings to flourish. They
have thrown aside ancient values
in return for instant gratification. They
have sold their souls to the highest bidder.
Take off your shoes stand before Me now –
not as sinners awaiting banishment, but
as sons and daughters who will help to
rebuild My world with Love.

18 June

Every mother's tears will be wiped dry.
I know her pain, I know her courage.

Whilst searching for herself, she gives
of herself to creation.

Each utterance of joy from her heart,
of Love for her young, echoes in the
halls of Heaven. Each act of selfless
Love has power.

19 June

My Light shall dispel all darkness,
even though many live in wickedness
and utter corruption.

As they draw their last earthly breath,
they will use it to call upon the One
whom they have cursed, for sacred
forgiveness.

Do not wait for the last moment, but kneel
before Me now, in your hearts, and in
your thinking, I will hear!

20 June

There is always a door in front of you.
Yours alone is the decision to open it,
or allow it to remain closed.

Yours too the decision whether to walk
through, or to remain still. But it is
impossible to remain still, for life's purpose
for all is to progress, to change!

Open the door with wonder, excitement,
anticipation, and discover what lies beyond!

21 June

Beyond all time and space, beyond all
understanding. But the human heart
and mind strives for greater connection.
There will always be situations that will
challenge, but you must hold firm
in your faith.

The Light that you have journeyed so far
to find will not now be extinguished.
It will not take back its brilliance.
And in that Light, see Me.

22 June

Beautiful are the days when you are
at peace with Me.

Wonderful is the joy known, when you
are in My company.
Therefore, seek this constantly, for it is
a 'soul' connection.

And it is that which all would strive to
attain.

23 June

You live in My house now, and no ill shall befall you. You are in My keeping.

My angels guard your every step. Safe and sure you will be, for you live in My Light now.

Open your heart to others; they suffer, for they do not know Me. They do not know My peace. Your Love will let them see another way to be – the *only* way to be.

24 June

So many occurrences threaten to take you from My path. All is but testing, all is but an illusion.

Know this: only Love is real. Protect yourself with Light; surround yourself with Love and be strong, in My name.

25 June

Rest now in Me. Take time to be still;
for all turmoil disrupts the calm soul.

Rest now in My Love, for only that
will return you to peace.

26 June

Let Me be at your side. Let Me help you
each step of the way. The journey is
rugged and fraught. Turn to Me,
the friend at your side. In all things, turn
to Me for help. Ask, and it shall be given.

Be the wise one, to whom others will turn.
Be the one who has a place in their heart
for those in need.
But do not let their lack of faith rob you
systematically of your energy or peace.
For you have a strength within that others
see, and would desire.

Guard yourself well with My Light. Then
you can be of more service, in My name.

27 June

Let the past dissolve into nothingness;
for to keep it alive is a false notion.

Remember, if you will, the joyful times;
otherwise let it go! Let all remain in the past.
The only answer is forgiveness!
For that conscious act can draw a line under
old battles, and will allow wounds to heal.

The present moment has the power to create.
Use it to live, to change, to progress!

28 June

Look to the Light, for it will dispel
all darkness. Look to the Light, for
it will illuminate your path.

When all is despair and there seems to
be no hope, look to the Light and know
that the Kingdom of God is all around
you.

29 June

Turn around, and know that I am there,
for I am Love – the Love which
creates, sustains and maintains.

Fear destroys.

In the history of civilisations,
fear has overtaken and overcome many times;
it has caused devastation, and the downfall
of mankind.

Only Love can rebuild!

30 June

I look favourably on those who call
My name, in prayer, in Love and in
thanksgiving.

For My name itself is a blessing.
My name soothes, protects and takes away fear.

And when in torment, doubt, or feeling
neglected and badly used, call upon My name,
for all healing is there.

1 July

Quieten those unruly thoughts;
gather them gently into a safe place,
as a loving shepherd would guide his sheep.

And in that place, be peaceful. For it is
with Me that you meet.

This is the important time; this is the only
place in which great things can be achieved.
Peace with Me is the first step.

2 July

Let your bruised heart recover!
Let your senses be calm!
In the midst of all turmoil, know that
I am with you there.

Go within now, and find that quiet place
in your deep heart. That place which is
beyond anyone and anything. And in
that place, find the courage that will help
you, in the face of all adversity.

3 July

Many judge without fact and without
compassion, ready to condemn
and pass sentence.

Woe betide the sinner who falls into
the hands of the unruly mob.
Woe betide those who look on.

Are they not also guilty, when they
stand by and allow evil to flourish?

In My name, find courage to act!

4 July

I am at the door of your hearts.
The Light of the world patiently awaits.
Those who seek will find Me; those who
try to live in My ways shall find peace.

The days are long and weary, when lived
without Me. Only those who have turned
their hearts to the Light do I invite
to the table.

Humanity is frail and takes time
to awaken. How can you fail to respond
now, when you know of My Love?
Each day, hear the call of service, the call
that mankind has waited so long to hear!

5 July

I came into the world to say, 'Love one another!' It is still the same, simple message. Your hearts are mine: do not fail Me!

It is a good thing, to be sensitive to others' needs and feelings. It is not good to be so hardened as not to hear the cries of those in distress.
Many are impervious to any intelligence beyond their own immediate knowing.

6 July

Walk each day with Me, as your closest companion.

Make a small, daily commitment.
Set a goal, and work towards it.
Be decisive, acting only in Love for others in My name.
See the good in all, for they too travel the path.

7 July

When you feel furthest away from Me,
that is the time to come into
My presence.

You know you must; for nothing else
will soothe a troubled heart. Let My
enfolding Love contain you, and slowly,
let all fears release.

Let My Light bathe your soul;
then gently, calmly, allow the restoration
of peace within.

8 July

Let the sun set, and as it disappears
beyond the horizon, so too let all of the
day's happenings. Let them all fade.

To carry over builds one event
upon the other, and becomes a burden.

Take from your day only sweet memories,
and create a place of joy,
wherever you are!

9 July

In My pure glory you stand. I delight
in this knowing.

For each one who comes to Me in Love for Me,
in joy of Me, touches the heart of
Heaven.

10 July

Together in My name. A force strong
and undivided, a force that is
unmatched.

Remember it is for Me that you work,
it is My name upon your banner!
So fear no one and nothing.

11 July

Glorious, abundant, perfect creation;
all merging, all interwoven.
All flowing, one into another, in perfect
Love.

Accept your part in this miracle
called life.

12 July

Act upon the good thoughts that you
have been given, as all is for positive
guidance. Act as soon as possible.

Do not let the sun set, unless you have
put good deeds into practice.

Time will steal away your days.
And the enemy – procrastination – leads to low
esteem, negativity and all that suggests ill.
Act now, in goodness, in Love –
and in My name.

13 July

To stand firm in My name...

To find courage, when all others flee.
To not forsake Me in the darkest hour.

These are the qualities of My friends.

14 July

Each day will present golden moments.

When a higher state of consciousness is achieved, through prayer and meditation, the time between each moment will dissolve...

thereby creating continuous awareness, of the greater gifts bestowed.

15 July

As a white dove, My peace shall descend.
And My words shall create harmony.

Mankind will not turn away from this
wisdom and beauty.

For it is that which they long to hear.
Their deepest hearts have cried out in
anguish. And they will recognise the
One who speaks;
for all will acknowledge Me.

16 July

Greater sensitivity is required, not only
for your own needs, but the needs of those
around you.

And if in this reality you can rise
beyond that which keeps you tied,
and slip the bonds of earth, all will be
possible. For you will have reached
unlimited awareness.

A being at one with all things,
you will slide between the worlds,
and touch the Universal Mind,
attaining a state of perfection, to enable the
Lord's work to be manifest.

17 July

Grief beyond bearing, give to Me.
Fear beyond description, give to Me.
Deeds beyond forgiveness, give to Me.
Wounds beyond healing, give to Me.

Lay all at My feet.
My Love will transform all into joy
beyond believing!

18 July

Only when you rest in Me will it be complete.

Only when you allow your soul a living freedom, will you know the truth.

19 July

Always with Me, always in My presence. Nothing can or will ever separate, for it was created so.

When separation exists in the minds of men, the illusion continues.

Think now to a time when all was well. Think now when your heart was full of Love for those dear to you.

The years pass, and all change. Look back in Love only, and look forward to a joyful tomorrow.

20 July

Suffer no more, for in My arms
only joy is there.

Innocent hearts will return from whence
they came. My plan for you is to Love only.
In My name, give all that you can,
and all that you are. Never flinch from
the task that I have set.

You have returned, in your heart, to Me.
I will not fail. It was you who walked
away. It was I who waited for your
homecoming.

Do not despair for it is all emotion. Once
recognised and understood for what it
truly is, you will be rock-steady, with Me!

21 July

Meet Me in a sacred place;
meet Me in your heart.
Let all confusion and pain slip away.
Let only clarity and truth light your path.

Know that actions and decisions, made in
Love only, and with the best of intentions,
are acceptable. There comes a time when all
have to choose. *The time is now!*
It is a question of dedicating your life to Me,
or ignoring this call.

Thousands have been called and given
their lives. I ask you, now, to come to Me.
Your way will become clear. Trust only
in a good outcome. When you come from
a lower perspective, the way will be clouded.
Look for the higher level. Look for the
highest outcome, for all concerned, in any
situation, and know that you will be
guided!

22 July

Where are you now? How far away from Me have your thoughts taken you?
How far has your daily routine interrupted your time with Me?

When will you come out from behind the mask? When will you believe in Me, and in yourself?

When will you stand firm and say,
'This is who I am.'?
And who are you?
You are the one from whom My Light shines – one in whom I put My trust!

23 July

This is a time of great healing. A time of discovery! A time of letting go of old ways.

Many will look to you for direction, for steadfastness, for positivity. You will acquire all of these and more, when you walk with Me.

Surround yourself with My Light, allow it to envelope all that you are. And all that you are is boundless, limitless and joyful!
All that you have been will merge, as you become more and more at one.

24 July

Only trust in Me, and you shall know such joy.

Only believe in all that has been given, and you shall know such peace...
No one can take that away.

25 July

And you will find Me,
for I am everywhere.

Let your mind expand and connect
with Divine Will.

Let your heart open, to absorb the
wonders of miracles witnessed.
Let your eyes see My glory.

26 July

All healing is just a thought away,
and let that thought be of Me.

Repeat My name as you would a prayer;
for My name holds power, peace and
Love.

Before time began, I was. In time, I am.
And in time eternal, I shall be.

27 July

And it will be as I have said.
All shall be responsible for their actions.

All shall search for their path of truth.
All will come to know Me and return home, at their appointed hour.

And I await them, but not alone. For hundreds, thousands rejoice, as each completes their journey.

28 July

They shall stand and wonder.
They will ask, 'Who is this?'

Understanding will be heard in their heads and in their hearts.

They will recognise the Divine Being.
They will know that I am amongst men once more.

29 July

Listen to the children.

They do not seek to falsify
for personal gain.

They come straight from Heaven's Light.
Purity, truth and wisdom
shall pour from their mouths.

30 July

As the sun arises and the dawn blesses
a new day, turn your hearts to Me
in thanksgiving.

For the heart, which is in constant
gratitude and in a mode of joy,
will be in receipt of generous bounties!

Let your lives be a reflection
only of Love.

31 July

Born a stranger, in a strange land...

But now a stranger no more; for you have come home!

Home to Me, in your heart.

1 August

Let all despondent thoughts float away.
They are capable of causing downfall,
if allowed to persist.

You must clear them from your mind
with determination.

Let them go, and in their place nurture
and take unto yourself thoughts and
glimpses of Me and higher realms.

2 August

A lone mother's tears cannot change
the world.

But as a vast army amassed that would
march across the landscape, the status quo
could be challenged.

For who would dare to stand in the face
of such a formidable force?
Let those who bear and nurture creation
unite in My name, for the sake of
goodness.

3 August

On your journey through life, let Me be your companion.

Together we shall walk, comfortably in each other's company, as old friends.

Let Me be the One to whom you turn spontaneously, in joy or sorrow.

4 August

There are many dark paths that need illumination, and many back alleyways of the mind that require more
than a little cleansing and whitewashing.

Many complex personality traits and layers of emotional baggage need to be healed and discarded.
All need recognition and acceptance.
All need facing and surrounding with Love.
Dissolve these blockages and move on.

5 August

Immeasurable, unfathomable! Far
beyond the capabilities of the human mind
are the workings of God's plan.

All is governed, all is predetermined,
within the concept of free will.
But ultimately, man's goal is to rise above
personality, emotional and the physical.

Problems and conflict are caused by
separation, for all are one, in the
knowledge and Love of God. Man's
journey is to experience and encounter
all things, until realisation allows the
soul's return to source!

6 August

Many times I have said, 'Call upon Me and I will hear.' Therefore, call upon Me. In your moments of delight or despair, know that I hear – before your words are formed.

At daybreak and at eventide, let your thoughts turn to Me. Let your hearts and minds dwell on the beauty and peace that I am.

Continued meditative practice will help you to become aware of another dimension. The existence of a higher self; of One that is connected to the Divine: a self that rests in an unlimited sea of Love.

7 August

Let the eternal sound of creation echo throughout your life.

Let it become a beautiful unbroken chord that all will recognise. Let it be all.

8 August

I am here in the Light; I am here in the shadows: see Me! And know that both are equal.

Direct your thoughts to Me.

Celebrate each day, for you will have attained a treasure beyond price – inner peace!

9 August

Rest now and ponder on all happenings.

Know that all is sent for guidance and healing.

Great has been your learning and wisdom gained.

10 August

Let closeness to Me remind you
of who you really are. Let tranquillity
pervade your being.
Your own will not hear, for they think
they know you; but they have little
knowledge of themselves.

Only your willingness
to serve will ensure a right outcome.
See all situations with Love and
compassion. For it is only the constant
changing of lines and scenes, in a
play within a play...

11 August

As waves perpetually wash the shore,
so My voice constantly calls to you.

Will you hear Me? Will you lay all aside,
and declare your allegiance to Me?

For I am your Lord.
I am the One who talks and walks with you:
know this to be true. Be still and
know this!

12 August

Tell Me now of all that ails, of all that
holds you back...

of all that which prevents you coming
to Me. Tell Me in your quiet moments
and in your prayers.

For I alone have the power to see through
the dense fog that surrounds you. Take
time to absorb this Divine guidance.

13 August

The work that must be done, in the
first instance, is within yourself.
For there is no other place to start.

It stands to reason that all will follow:
peace, joy and wisdom, in abundance.

But it is not an easy task, for the mind
will resist efforts to cease its chatter.

14 August

Always strive to seek the truth!
It stands clearly for all to see.

Although many would deny and
hide, it can never be disguised
completely.

I am the way, the truth, the life:
seek these things, and see Me.

15 August

Give to others your Love. Give all
that you have. For joy is created in the most
wondrous of ways, when Love is shared!

Such generosity brings the warmth of
the sunshine, and is remembered with
fondness.

It reflects in the lives of all those who receive,
and it continues to flow. Golden
and precious are the days filled with Love.

16 August

How beautiful the time when you
withdraw from busy, chaos-filled days!
How beautiful, as your thoughts become
lighter and more focused.

You see now only a small portion of the
picture. Each day more and more will
be revealed, more and more will be understood.

Not all will want to commit. They want
their lives for themselves. Not all would
wish to give selflessly.

17 August

They shall speed at My command,
for they do My bidding.

Angels of Love, healing and peace —
they appear when needed.

Their desire is to comfort and protect.
Tune in to their wondrous energy!

18 August

No more pain, no more tears.
I have heard your prayers.
I have heard your calls,
and will make you whole.

Then let joy and thanksgiving fill your lives.
Send away now any thoughts of sadness;
turn despair away from your hearts.

Ask only for help; know all comes from Me.
All shall come to Me; there is not one
who will not do so. Here for a while,
and then to return: it was always thus!

19 August

All, in their own way, are as children who cry alone in the dark.

But in no time at all, perception can change. All can become Light.

The thought that you are one with Me will illume your whole existence.

20 August

I would have you know that all is Love.

I would have you understand that there is no separation. Heart and soul are one with Me.

To withhold love from another is to withhold love from yourself. And yet, you would only wish Love for yourself.

All are valuable, all make their own contribution; comparisons therefore have no substance.

21 August

If your fellow man should stumble, reach out your hand to steady him.

Reach out your heart, with Love.

You surely recognise yourself. For all stumble, all falter. All have heart wounds, all know desolation.

Reach out, in My name, with words of comfort.

22 August

It is now time. For in My name, you go out into the world!

It is now time to shake off the old and put on the new.

It is now time to profess your Love for Me.

23 August

Awaken now to the Love that is yours to receive. I am here, and would infuse your very soul with Light and beauty, beyond any known.

Here lies the doorway to bliss, awaiting opening. Here lies all joy, all knowledge. For you will know that you are one with Me. Therefore, all that is mine is yours.

Your joy will radiate to others; for they will see that you have a gift beyond price. A gift freely given to those who search, to those who ask.

24 August

Today is all you have. Moments passed are simply that. Each moment presents itself as the future. Each moment is valuable, for it allows choice.

Do not stand idly by, when My little ones cry out in pain and hunger. For cruelty has rocked their lives and taken their joy. Harshness has replaced Love.

Do not stand with ears closed to the sounds of distress; you must do what you can. Walk hand in hand, and share your blessings. Each act of kindness is noted. Each word of comfort given is heard and magnified – for others are touched.

25 August

Already in My keeping are those
whose hearts are mine.
Held gently and in My Love, sleeping,
are those who have come home. No toil
or fret can change this; no anxious care
will alter it.

Take comfort, for with Me they rest. This
knowledge rolls away the tombstone;
this intelligence sets all free.

26 August

In this world, there is no other help.
All is gone, all is confusion;
all sight blinded, direction unobtainable.
When fear alone runs through your veins,
there is no other course of action but to
come to the only place where Love abides.

My child, rest now; for in My glory would
I cover you, in My Light would I hold you.
Struggle and exhaustion is near
completion; peace and joy are yours to behold.

Who can tell the measure of trials? Who
knows, but Me? And from Me, such strength
comes when least expected,
when Love and patience are aroused,
not anger or frustration.
When such a level of understanding is attained,
you have crossed the threshold!

27 August

In each age there comes One, but now there are many. Those of the Light will be creators of miracles!
They will instigate changes of perception in hearts and minds. For men will know that there can be no other way!

All that ever has been, and all that is to come is only the result of thought.
Instigate right action now with thoughts of Light, to create a world fit for My children. Old ways of being will fade, to allow the birth of the new!

28 August

The personality must be quietened, the
ego must be calmed!
All must be in balance.
This is individual work. All stand alone
until oneness has been achieved.

And you are one with Me. All abundant
life is yours for the understanding, the
asking, the accepting!
The search is over, the journey into bliss
begins. As soon as you know, you
want for nothing.

29 August

Take charge of your thoughts. They constitute what and who you believe yourself to be, and therefore, what you attract. Train them in the arena of positivity to create in your life. To allow anything else is to invite confusion.

Now welcome! For I bid you come into My presence. Be at peace, and allow all the day's turmoil and anxiety to fade.
My peace! Is it not just a breath away?
Is it not the merest thought that you know can change? I am unchanging, for ever, until all eternity.
Focus on Me. Focus on what is real.

30 August

The voice of reason speaks clearly to you,
yet you refuse to hear. You will not
listen, for the pull of ego is so strong.

The voice has a wise and loving message.
Learn to trust it, for it is a part of you!

Wherever you are, whatever the
circumstance, all is in place for a reason.
It is to experience, and to move on!

31 August

Clear the last remnants of dark, dusty
corners from your mind!

Spring clean your life, until there are
no shadows wherein fear and painful
memories can hide.

Work at bringing in the Light,
and making all things as new. For with the
Light, there is only Love. And only in
Love have I sought you, and will guide you
home.

1 September

Constant and sure are My words.

These are given to you, to free you from
fear; to illuminate your path, and to
guide your every move.

Like a loving father who keeps His door open
for the sound of His child, I am
here!

I am your comforter, your protector,
your friend!

2 September

I come in unexpected ways.
I tread not the obvious path.
For you would be prepared, and would
treat Me in a false way.

I come as the stranger, the unlovable,
the one who would push you to your
limit.

I come to challenge in unusual situations,
for I am in all of these, and more! When
you see Me there and know only Love,
we walk as one.

3 September

The journey knows no end, for all
partake. All experience. Let the heavy
clouds disperse, for they obscure your
understanding. They hide the wondrous
blessings, which are yours by right!

And now I know that you have heard,
for your thoughts are with Me. I know
you have opened your heart, and your life
is now dedicated to Me.
The sleeper has been awakened. There is
nothing to forgive, nothing to fear.
For if all is Love, it knows not these.
Accept now what is offered, for it is given
without reservation, and in Love only.
Question not, for it is a truth!

4 September

Ask for the path to be shown.
Ask in all ways – in continuous joy,
thanksgiving, in prayer and in
silence. Ask, for an answer will come.

There will be many times when you feel
there has been no response. You will feel
deserted, but this is not so.
Remember, My child, that I see and know
all. I only have care for your greatest
good. Another way is being sought, for
the highest good of all concerned.

5 September

Search for Me, but not in crowded places,
for I am not there.
I am to be found in silence; I am to be
found in the sounds of creation.

And in the morning, there shall be
rejoicing, for My children have come home.
There shall be the rebirth of hope.
They will gather together, to support and
give strength to one another.
So be not discouraged, for now is the time
of trials. Now is the time to choose truth!

6 September

How best may you serve? How best may I
help you? Both are the same, because we
are one.

We, in the spirit of truth and Love, all
serve and help each other. Take now all that is
offered, in joyous acceptance – giving and
receiving...

It is as natural as breathing!

7 September

Surrender all that you think you have. Cast away all your illusions. Come into the only reality. For it is here, when you are alone, that I can speak with you best.

Do not hesitate to instigate quiet moments such as these. Solitude is the most perfect of partners, the most agreeable of companions. Hurry not back into the noise, for discordant sounds disturb the soul. Hurry only into My presence, My truth! For it is during these times that the greatest work is done.

Know this, and live this joy, for it is rare! In the stillness, wait for Me to give words of wisdom, hope and comfort, to all who search for such as these.

8 September

Connect now with a beautiful Light. Visualise and sense its brilliance! Bring it into your awareness. For this Light is a part of who you are, and a part of who you are becoming. As you breathe gently, imagine a rainbow of colours enveloping you in delicate shimmers. Allow these colours to permeate all that you are, and all that you are becoming. Continue to breathe gently. Within this meditative state, surround yourself with all that you wish to bring into your existence.

Cover all of this with Light and colours. Use positive emotions and sounds to enhance and play imaginatively. Focus on what you desire. It is a part of who you are, and a part of who you are becoming.

Breathe gently.

9 September

Await My words with joyous anticipation,
for they are your very life's blood. As I
call to you across the centuries, know
that time and space are as nought.
You are awakening from a dream, into reality.
But what is the truth? For you are the dream.

Seek your soul. It awaits your call.
It slumbers deeply, and needs constant attention.
The rewards of this work surpass imagination.
Serenity and bliss will take over.
Your personality will not be submerged,
but evolved. This is individual work. There is
service, in supporting others along this path.
But in solitude, know your own being.

10 September

And in this quiet place, hear only
My voice. As step by step, little by little,
you have been shown the way.

I guide through the twists and turns
of life's highway.

But in a moment all will be made clear,
all confusion understood; for the portal
opens slowly and steadily.

It is time now to go through, for the Light
that beckons is of Me.

That light shows you the way home.

11 September

Many live in such ignorance, such
darkness, they do not know that there
is a Light to which they can turn.

They are unaware that the Light is
within.

It may take a fall from grace.
Such an event may precipitate a search for Light,
for truth!

12 September

I ask only for the simple soul, the
gentle spirit, to come.

My work is not for the great ego, or
those who are dedicated to worldly
glory.

I ask for those who are willing to
undergo all manner of trials, in My name.
I ask for you.

13 September

My words flow through you, for the good of all concerned.

Let your mind be peaceful, let all anxieties fade. For it is during these times a greater connection is made, and direction given.

The day will come when there will be none other than this.

14 September

In evil's clutches no more, for you have chosen Me.

No more pain or misunderstanding,
for you have sought the only alternative.

Walk now with purpose!

Your way is clear, and you walk it
with Me.

15 September

Let not your faith be torn asunder.
at the first sign of difficulties.
There are those who would
be glad at your downfall.

Stand firm, and let yourself
be surrounded with Light.

Just believe that all things are possible
with God. Nothing, and no one can
stand against Him. So little is their
time to rejoice that you could have pity on them,
for they know not.

Know that all is well... all shall be well!

16 September

One by one they join Me, for they have returned to the only Love.

One by one shall their hearts accept My truth.

And who shall be afraid, when their hour comes? Only those who know Me not. But I have told you, My resurrection overcame death, with a Love to conquer all fear!

17 September

Ask, and it shall be given; ask, and it shall be shown. For all is Mine to bestow. All are as one in My name. All are as a single thought. When the moment comes, you will know; for I will send knowledge of what is required.

Much testing of the spirit has been put into place, many trials have been endured. But you turned to Me, you never forsook the One who loves you.
Be therefore at peace, child of mine; be still and know.

18 September

Leave the everyday busy, busy work,
the distractions. They take you
further and further away from Me.

The only work now is to find the road
back into My presence.

My heart recognises your efforts. For it
is when you give of your true self, in
selfless service, that is the most worthy.

Then you will know Me, and there will
be no need for any other.

19 September

In My name only, live your life. For
your life is Mine – we are one!
Together as friends, together as co-creators,
together for all time.

Do not doubt, do not let fears
in the dark night unnerve you.

Walk fearlessly into the day, knowing
that I am with you.

20 September

Come into My dwelling place.
Come into My Love.
Know that no person who has sought
the Kingdom has been refused.

For entry is a Divine right. Entry is
automatic, for you are already there.
The understanding takes you.
It is instantaneous, it is within.

21 September

Hear Me now, for the words I give are
uplifting and sure! I will speak now to you
and to all who will read.
Know that I am the only truth. In Me only
will you find the way home –
the home from whence you've travelled.

There is a world beyond any that you can
ever imagine. A place of peace
and beauty, as yet undefined by any
description. Such Love and joy, that all
creation would instantly acknowledge –
this is where we would lay our heads.

This is the world of the eternal. This is
the Heavenly place that is the reality.
The earth upon which you tread is but
the dream from which you will awaken.

22 September

Let your steps be unfaltering.
Even in the midst of all turmoil, you
know your path.

It was set long before the dawn of time,
long before the mountains came into
being. Knowing this, what could ail you?

Therefore, let only thankfulness and
gladness be your watchwords. Live in
the Light of these.

23 September

I will gladly speak, knowing
that you will gladly listen. Knowing
that you make time for silence, in which to
hear.

Many call upon Me, and know not
the power in their supplication.

Your prayers won't go unanswered. I will
rescue you from all division and discord.
Think only of Me to know this. I am
ever present, so be at peace.

They will come from all regions to hear,
for great is your faith.

24 September

In great multitudes they come –
the unseen forces of the Light.
In great Love and awareness, they do
what is agreed.

So beautiful, so gentle, that words
are not enough. But know that they
serve Me. And mankind has need of
such as these.

And who could ask for more? All that
is mine to give is given, in Love for
you only!

25 September

Did I not say, I would speak with you?
Did I not say, I would come in all ways?

So be ready, be ever watchful, for even
up to the end, there will be tests.
They are not to outwit or dismay, but to
ensure your heart's Love for Me.
And for those who overcome, the rewards of
these trials are sweet; the coming into
My presence, glorious!

26 September

The way will be made clear, for
each day the Light shines brighter!

Each moment, a star is born to
illuminate the darkness. Look not to
past struggles. Know that one thought of Me
is sufficient to heal all discord.

Many do not see; they look for glory,
fame and wealth. But that is not how
I work, that is not for My true hearts.

27 September

My heart only knows Love.
My wisdom reflects the highest,
and both I impart to you!

No evil shall befall you, therefore rejoice.
Now accept blessings; they fall as gently
as summer rain.

Silently, plentifully and wondrously,
they cover all aspects of your life;
no area is unaffected.

28 September

You will know that I am there. For to
know Me, is to see Me in all things –

I dance in every ray of sunshine,
every rainbow, and in each life-sustaining
moment.

You will know Me!

29 September

I will gladly help those who ask, for I
cannot refuse. I will never turn away.

For My Love is there, for all.

Boundless joy and ceaseless praise
will be your natural state, as connection
with Me strengthens.

30 September

All is well, for in My house you rest.
The day begins and ends with Love.

The journey continues, and who knows where it leads?

Take the road that leads only to Me!

1 October

Tender are the mother's thoughts for the child. Tender are My thoughts, for you! A watchful Love and care is ever present.

In this world and beyond, there is no difference!

2 October

Walk with Me now, feel My presence, all around you.

Open your eyes and see a reality, open your heart and know another. For we are one and Heaven is where you are now.

When I am ready, I will call you. I will let you know all that you have to do in My name. So rest gently now.

3 October

Born again, each day anew,
to experience and to seek Me!

Born again, until you experience
only Me!

4 October

A Love greater than any known,
has been lain at your feet. Will you accept it?
Will you bend your knee, and take it
carefully to yourself? I await your sign,
your acknowledgement.

Let all thoughts of controlling others go.
For it cannot be; no one has jurisdiction
over another. Step back and know this.
Now allow a peaceful conclusion of your day.
In silence, communicate your hopes
and your fears to Me. Your heart will
reveal all secrets, for all is known.
All stand before the throne. Recognition of
true worth is a natural process. Do not
despair, for where can Love be hidden?

5 October

The power of Love is greater than any of the forces of darkness.

So trust now that My Love goes with you always, in all situations.

6 October

To let Me help you with your burden is for you to help Me with mine.

My cross becomes lighter, as those with awareness step up and take hold. And so with you.

Take hold of the troubles that burden others, and make them lighter. Make My heart lighter, make the world lighter!

7 October

Where will you look? Where will your next distraction appear? There will be countless, and you will tire.

For only when you realise that you search for Me, will your search be over. And then the journey begins.
Look to each golden moment, for therein lies My truth.

All will be revealed. For one moment builds upon another, and will become the joyous day. Look now to each other and seek recognition.

8 October

You will be amazed when the miracle
happens. For you have entrenched
yourself in yesterday's pain and unbelief.

And yet I say, all can be changed in an
instant. For the thoughts that hold you back
are only made of clouds
that hide the sun.

But yours alone must be the turning,
away from the dark, and the choosing
of the Light. This must be a conscious
step, and becomes the miracle!

9 October

Know that Love has been captured for all time, held in trust by pure hearts, to be released into the world when the need is greatest.

Know that Love has been secured, held in trust, by gentle souls, to be shared amongst many.

Stir now, do not stand back in idleness. For these are your days, given that you might rise to action... given so that you might be the Love that is created and held, so that others might become secure.

10 October

Take unto yourself only that which is of Me, for all else is but false. All else is not to be trusted. Let your instincts guide you in all your dealings, for many set out to deceive, and have only their own interests at heart. All have this to a certain degree, but it is the inflated ego that will inflict the most harm.

Take your strength from wisdom gained over many years, from many sources. Harden not your heart, for openness is one of the greatest gifts. Being able to give and accept Love is fundamental to humanity's growth. Let sincerity and truthfulness be your guides on the path through life. For one supports the other. Above all, Love! For Love drives out the terrors created by fear. Love allows the Light to flow! It will dispel the darkness. Love alone will Light your way home.

11 October

Be vigilant, for there are those who would
ensnare you. There are 'thought-forms' that
would dislodge and cause chaos.

Steady and continued practice of prayer
and meditation will serve its purpose –
which is to strengthen the will and
bring about positivity and calmness.
This is the only individual and collective
way to progress towards being.

12 October

Praise and thanks gladden My heart!
And so the world is uplifted.

A thought or deed, created in My name,
with no expectation of reward, is of the
highest.

For it is Love, and Love's circles expand
with each pure act. Love's circles enfold,
more and more.

13 October

Put your trusting hand into mine,
and know that I will guide you safely
home.

Yours is not to be disturbed or fretful.
Yours is to know that all is working out.

All is in order for the best outcome. When
many are of one mind, for the good of all,
the results can only be blessed.

14 October

The world's noises and confusions
still clamour for your attention.

The pull to be involved is very strong.
But the pull towards My peace must be
even stronger.

The power of good, which can be achieved
when you are at one with Me, and come
from a serene and Loving centre, knows
no bounds. Limitless and miraculous can
be the achievements.

Love is the ultimate healer!

15 October

There is no other answer than to turn your attention to Me.

All your moments, your hours, your days – together we will overcome any difficulty. If you ask help of Me in any way, I will be there.

I only ask that you be still and hear.

16 October

And in your hour of need, help will come…

For the very desire will bring Me to your side.

Your day is but young, and has yet to unfold its glory.

17 October

Struggles abound, for it is the earthly path.
Do you not see? Why has it to be
the way you think best? There are reasons
why it is as it is.

Guard well your heart. Keep it free from
unloving ways. Guard well your hopes
and dreams, for they are a part of the journey
of self-discovery.

Surround all that you are with a golden Light.
Let this beauty protect you,
in ways that nothing else can.

18 October

Stop, and take yourself to task when
you try to live without Me. For all
eventually realise it cannot be done.

I am the way, the truth, the life. As
said of old, as stands firm today.

Millions will come to know, and in this
knowledge they will rejoice. For it is My
Love to which they return.

19 October

And My way shall unfold, all will
become clear. All those who know
will help the lonely, dejected soul.

All those who work for Me will pray
together, for Light to enter, where there
now is only darkness and desolation.
Pray in God's name that such as these
will turn and choose the Light.

Pray that they will see the glimmer
of a distant star, and make it their own!

20 October

Love must surely triumph, and only
right action will bring about Love.

Tears, grief and regret are but futile;
what is required is right action!

Make your decision and stay with it.
Be courageous; ask of Me all that you need,
and I will hear! How long the night,
when the morning refuses to come.

21 October

Connect with Divine Will, and every outcome will be of the highest.

Connect with Me, before speech, before action. Take a breath – a Divine breath – and allow My Love to fill your whole being.

22 October

Not yours to know.
Not yours to work out,
for it cannot be accomplished.

Tread your path lightly.

23 October

Do not give up hope, for it is your very
life's blood. It pulses through the veins
and swells the heart.

Hope keeps going when all else is gone.
Hope holds all together. Courage, Love,
strength and faith – these are the flowers.

Hope is the gentle shower of rain
that encourages them to grow.

24 October

Your faith will be rewarded, your Love
and persistence will see good returns.

Do not be afraid; for what is it? It is
but thought!

But also, do not be deceived. Thoughts
are powerful, for good or ill. However
they are expressed, they create a result.

25 October

Here they come – the Messengers of
the Light! With purpose and joy,
they make themselves known to you.

With Love they surround you.
Make this a day in which to behold their
nearness. Make this a day in which
to be thankful.

26 October

Why do you doubt, why are your fears
overtaking all other?

Take hold of the situation now, act only
in goodness. Act only for the best outcome
of all concerned. Help is always at hand.

I will send what is needed.

27 October

Now I know that we walk together,
for you have acknowledged My presence.

Never again will fears, on any level,
cause tremors which unnerve and block
progress!

28 October

Infused with spirit, you can now only
go on.

Infused with determination and energy,
you can now only succeed.

For even in times of your greatest peril,
you sought Me, and knew Me to be there!

29 October

Cover yourself with courage, for it is
a good and sturdy armour.

Have ready in your hand the sword
of righteousness, for with it you can
protect all truth!

Place upon your head a helmet of Light,
and thus adorned, be fearless!

30 October

'Let not your heart be troubled!
Neither let it be afraid.' All is
just a passing dream, and as such
will fade when the morning comes.

Your Love will bring about the
miracle that you have asked for.

31 October

Those that gather in My name
are dear to Me.

For they support and encourage each other
through difficult and dark days.

The energy thus generated creates such
Love, such joy. Radiance expands,
and they will become known.

1 November

You walk a long and lonely path,
unrecognised by those around.

Give some of the Love, which you would
willingly share with others, to yourself.

Give some of the consideration and
respect, which you so readily give to
others, to yourself.

Now be aware that although you walk
the same path, you now wear a protective
coat of Love. And feel secure.

2 November

When a heart reaches out in Love
to touch another, it will ignite a spark of
recognition.

A heart which hitherto was covered over
by the weight of the world...

That spark, if allowed, may become bold –
and with encouragement, may grow into
a beautiful flame! Heart to heart, thus
will the world be healed.

3 November

Tell them of your experience. Let them know what it is like to have such a personal connection with the Father of all.

Many have come to tell, in different ways. This is your way! Your way has been trust, Love and dedication. Know that I have been with you.

Let Me encourage you, in order to encourage others. For even if one soul is helped, one soul set upon a different path, one soul who will then help another, it will have been worth every moment!

4 November

The outer shell is bombarded from
every direction; wounds strike deep,
and your heart is sore. Your system closes
down, in order to protect you from further hurt.

All have felt thus; all contemplate and try
to reason. But answers will not come, for
there simply are none. The only course of
action is, in silence, to seek Me. Call Me,
and tell Me of your pain.
My Love will soothe all hurts, and you will
know that this is the answer.

5 November

How quickly you forget Me.
How quickly you allow old fears to swallow up
all that you are. Find strength to stay on
your path, find courage, for it is there.
If you fight for Me, in My name, then
fight with all your being. Stay constant
and true, knowing that I walk with you!

You were brought here to shine, and shine
you must. A Light to which others will look.
Their eyes will see a beauty, and a
gentleness, for you share My nature.
They will know that this is the only way to live.

6 November

A quiet, but determined, witness for Me.
A quiet, but dedicated life – to My glory.

For when all else is banished from the
heart and mind, only Love will reside
there.

Perfect Love casts out fear!

7 November

One day out of thousands will seem different.

One day will change all that you have taken for granted.

The day is coming when you declare your allegiance to Me. Your life will no longer be run on 'normal' lines; no longer lived within 'accepted' parameters.

There will be no mistaking the day.

8 November

Can you start to imagine how it can be?
Can you feel yourself there? Can you see
yourself as you would like to be?
Can you imagine yourself
surrounded by love, joy, prosperity?
All that you desire in abundance. It is on the
inner that you must begin, so commit yourself
to do this work.

Visualise how you would like it to be;
see yourself in that situation. Act it out in
your mind, laugh with pleasure at the
scenes of Love played out. Take time to
make this the most important work in your life.

For the law of attraction is strong. What
you give out in your deepest heart and
soul, you will get back. You will attract
events, people and circumstances into
your life, to reflect what is happening for
you. These things teach you about yourself.

9 November

Receive unto yourself a blessing.
Receive acknowledgement for all that
you have achieved.

It is noted and not forgotten. Many
Love you, and would give recognition
for your courage and strength of character.
These days have been testing times. All on
the path must struggle so. It is not until the
struggle is relinquished that the battle
is won. For you then rest in Me!

10 November

It is not for you to predict outcomes,
for all is in My keeping. Yours must be
to give it all up to Me, and trust.

Yours is but a tiny walk-on, walk-off
part in the play of life.

It is so for all; each part makes up
the whole. Not one could stand alone!

11 November

There can be no ease, no settling, no rest, until you exist completely in My Love.

I alone direct your comings and goings.
Ask of Me, each day, for guidance; it will be given.

12 November

Searching, searching...
Always searching! But do you not know you search in vain? For your search is directed on the material, and on the current situation.

But there is no need to look further, for all security lies within you.

Be still, and allow your glory to uncover.
Allow peace and Love to manifest from within!

13 November

Walk with Me now, in My beautiful
garden. For here is rest, here is peace!
Here is the tranquillity that you long
to discover.

Walk with Me now, knowing that all is well.
For when you sever bonds that tie,
that act alone unites you with Me.
Walk with Me now, as your friend and guide,
and all else will flow;
for you will experience a greater Love,
a greater understanding!

14 November

And there shall come One who will make himself known to all men. One who is already amongst you. Many are beginning to know this, but not in great numbers. The day will dawn when all will know Him.

He has come to remind you that all are brothers. All will learn that they must live in a different way – a way that is based on peace and Love.

Many have made money their God.
It was not meant to be.
For I alone am God. All will come to know this. It is in My name that you receive this, and in My name will you tell all others who would hear!

15 November

Oh, gentle child! My hand upon your brow.
All that you have been, all you are
is known by Me,
all thoughts, all deeds recorded.

For each one, the moment of homecoming
is a revelation. When covered
in earthly dilemmas, turmoil and
confusion, these things only serve to
distance you from My peace.

The moment of homecoming is when
you give up all of these and are only
surrounded with Love. Know that it is
there; feel it, live it! Be joyous for your
blessings. You have walked the dark night
but now the morning has come!

16 November

You will meet with others, and their
Love will help you overcome
great challenges.

For this is what it is about. You will be
supported, as you would support others.
And who can tell where the Love reaches?
None but I!
For an action, a thought, travels far
beyond your dreams, far beyond your
imagination!

17 November

A Light to guide your way will appear,
when you feel the most lost.
A hand to hold, when you feel most alone,
will reach out and say, 'I am with you.'

A heart that understands will make itself
known; a heart that has travelled the
same road; a heart that is of an Elder
who has gone before and who knows the
precarious journey.
All need such as these. All will enter
to those who are willing to be aware.

19 November

Make your decision to change, to heal,
this very instant.
There need not be special circumstances
in place before anything can happen.

It only needs the awareness that it
can be accomplished, and your allowing
every second of every day! This gift is
there, awaiting your acceptance.
This is the door upon which I say, 'Knock!'
It will be opened. This is the instant in
which you choose to live with Me.

18 November

You stand at the crossroads, with indecision paramount! Complicated challenges beset you and surround all paths. And yet, have faith that you will be guided. For all face such as these; all will find their way home.

Let go of all fear. Let go of old pain and draw to yourself only Love! Surround yourself with a cloak of Light, a cloak of spiritual protection, and be safe within. Know that no one, and nothing, can ever harm you. Know that you are of the Light, and all Heaven will protect you.

20 November

Before you, I stand. Will you let Me count you as My own? Will you take Me into your heart?

Before you, I stand as one who waits. As one who prepares a feast for your return, to My Love.

Before you, I stand – sure in the knowledge that your love for Me will overcome all obstacles, all manner of negative complications.

21 November

A beautiful, calm, clear Light enfolds you. Your heart and soul now need to open again and see this.

Take all from these days as difficulties to be overcome in My name. Know that rarely again will you be so tested! From now on, in any situation, seek Me in the first instance.
For I am Alpha and Omega, and in all things. Rejoice that it is so!

22 November

The passing of all those dear to you is but
that – a passing. They pass, not into oblivion,
but into an altered state of being. Their
energy stays intact throughout eternity.
That energy can evolve, wherever it is,
on whatever level.

All have choice. All are co-creators with Me.
All can choose fear or Love. It is the absence
of Love that creates space for fear to enter.
So now let peace pervade. Be at rest. Let Love
pervade. Let only Love be in your heart.

One with such knowledge, such compassion,
can only be as this. Others will follow your
direction, for they are lost and unsure.
Be steadfast in your ways, and know
that this is the truth.

23 November

Magnificent creation, a being of Love, a being of Light. All are such as these. All are on a journey, to awaken to the remembrance of this.

When words fail, actions will tell your story. Actions that are unadulterated and from the heart will be recognised as the most genuine and sincere. Simple actions of Love will be remembered long after the echoes of sounds have died away! So let your deeds speak volumes. Let your work create Love, let your hands create your heart's guidance.

24 November

A mighty force strikes at the very fabric
of your being.

Recognise the signs, and visualise a
golden light around you.
For energies are attracted to you,
and would steal away, with all that you are.

Work steadfastly, and know that you
can protect yourself. Remember that
Love alone will be your guard!

25 November

In all your days, remember Me.
For I am the Love of which you are a
part. I am the source from which you
have travelled.

I alone have guardianship of your soul.
I alone have the keys of all knowledge.
The keys to the gateway of everlasting bliss
are in My keeping. Cease your
struggle! Surrender now, and put your
life into My hands; and I will guide you
home.

26 November

A painful past and fearful future would, if allowed, destroy your *now*.

And now is all that you can experience. For now is all you have. It is also your moment of choice.

27 November

Come to Me. Let My Love wash over you! Let the power of the Divine Presence flow through you now, and restore lost energy.

Let it restore lost hope and vision, for there is nothing like this. Nothing in this earthly realm that can align itself with Me.

And when you finally come into that place, where there is only Love, you will know no other way of being.

28 November

Sweet and lovely are the moments
spent in My company.

A balm to the tortured soul, a soothing draught
to the tempestuous heart.
And when those who have suffered
enough come to realise they need only
turn and ask for healing Love, from a
never-ending supply, the sweet moments
become the continuous day.

29 November

And it is in these times that your heart
will break open. And when it does, be thankful!

For it is the allowing of all that has held
it closed to escape. The clearing of the
hardness that creates blockages will let
your tears flow and wash all clean.

As a mountain stream leaves no pebble
untouched by its pure water, so too your heart
will be cleansed and healed.

The healing will allow My presence to enter.

30 November

Where is Love? For it cannot be found. It has become a casualty in the search for an answer.

Where is truth? It lies buried beneath confusion and pain, caused also by the search.

Look not anywhere, but in silence; only there will you discover what you seek. For all Love and truth are there, and will reveal themselves to you.

1 December

Feel My presence with you now, for in your heart I reside.
Feel My Love with you now; allow no other but this.

Each tear is held sacred, when shed for Love of another.
Each thought and deed held worthy in My sight, when in purity created.

Share with Me all that you are, for it takes courage to live your truth.

2 December

We begin to see each other more clearly.
As the barriers to understanding fall away.

Know Me in your heart instead of your head,
and all will become clear to you.

Minds have reasoned and have tried to
box in that which cannot be held. Hearts
will heal, when they acknowledge Love is there.
For hearts will burst in joy and gratitude.
They have been smothered for so long.

To know this is to live without darkness;
fear is conquered. To really know this
is to live with the Love that I am.

3 December

Be gentle with yourself and others, for
the journey of life takes its toll.

Be gracious in all situations, and know
that many look to you for inspiration.
Be uplifted by the Love that you see in all.

Only let the Love that you have for Me
guide your actions.

4 December

Give God a chance.

Give the Love that He is, and that you are,
chance to live and grow. Accept
the miracle that you have prayed for.

Reach out your heart's compassion
to those whose eyes swell with tears of
sorrow. For you know and you recognise.

But you have risen above; you can no
longer be as you once were.

5 December

The life that is lived in service.

The eyes that see the Divine in all
things.

The heart that will not harm another
belongs to the one who is Mine!

Be the life, the eyes, the heart!

6 December

Inasmuch as you walk a straight course,
insatiable are they who would
drive you into seemingly inescapable
corners and alleyways. Let courage and
perseverance unite and see you through
the long night.

Let thoughts flow as in a peaceful stream.
Let turbulent and disturbing fears
now become calm.

All must, and will, experience extremes –
and all in between. For no matter what the
awareness attained, it is the stuff of life.
It is the human condition.

Throughout it all, direct your day-to-day
decisions, your way of being, towards
peace and Love; then rest there, with Me.

7 December

Servant of Mine, who sent you?
Know that it is Me.
Child of Mine, who would care and provide?
Know that it is Me.

Trust and give yourself completely into
that Love. Know that your every breath,
your every move, is purposeful.
And know that it is Me.

8 December

The world of your unseen guardians
awaits. The company of the highest
are at your door. Will you open it a little
further?

Will you invite them to come in? It is
good that you do, for all Love is there.
All help, in whatever form it might take,
is waiting to be showered upon you.
Trust in Me; but first, seek peace
within your own heart.

9 December

I give to you all that you would wish
for yourself. For all is there, awaiting
your desire of it.

Step out of these clothes and these shoes,
for they serve you no longer. A new robe
is there, for you to reach out and take hold of.
And when adorned, you will know who you are.
You will know the truths of the ages.

For yours are the gifts that have been
given to few. Use them wisely, use them
to be of assistance to those in need.
In all of this, be aware of your own self.
You walk surrounded by Light and Love.

10 December

Oh, glorious and beautiful day! A new
beginning, to know Me. No grand
situation is required to be in place;
each moment can unfold gently.
Let your thoughts be as seeds, each one
planted with Love. Nurture and train
them until they are strong and vibrant!
Care for them, until they are capable of
standing without support; for thoughts,
although not visible, are very real and
have potent energy.

Unless checked and guided, negativity
can be an overpowering weed
that will choke and distort.
So in wisdom, choose to create a beautiful
flower garden, where you may ever dwell
peacefully.

11 December

Nothing false, nothing forced! Only
gentleness and true Love of one
who is of Me.
For in My name you searched, and I
came to you, with the haste of One who
would gather to safety His own child!

Your plea has been heard,
and throughout all your trials you have
remained close.
I acknowledge that in truth and purity,
you will support and encourage many others
on their journey home.

12 December

No man stands alone; for all are brothers in My sight.

All know this at a deep level. But ego would deny Love, and a lack of Love manifests its opposite: *fear*.
Fear comes in multiple ways and creeps on and on, until Love is smothered.

Recognition of this is the first step to salvation. The next is the overcoming of fear – with Love.

13 December

Time passes so slowly, when you are
not engaged in My work. My work is of
the positive, the joyful, the nurturing.

Time will not hang heavy on your hands,
when, complete in your own self, you are
then able to see others' distress, others' pain,
and can offer support.

Not in the role of one who would take over,
but as a friend, who would allow
what is; a friend who stands at the
gate, knowing the moment of need.

14 December

Fundamental to well-being is the feeling of trust.
Trust in self, family, friends – and to a
larger extent, the community.
Ultimately, the trust in a higher power.
For one responds to another,
and one reflects another.
An individual who no longer trusts in anything,
let alone himself, is thrown into turmoil.
A sense of well-being is then sought,
to be captured from outside.
This can come in every form
of addiction known to man.
All chaos ensues, for the simple reason
that addictions are insatiable.
But one answer shouts louder than any other.
Cease searching on the outer
and look to the inner world.
Only with work done there,
through connection with Me,
will a difference be made.
Trust and peace in heart and soul
will be restored.

15 December

Welcome to the bright dawn of a new day!
Welcome to the birth of a new moment!
Rejoice at their coming, for it is the
affirmation of My Love for you. You are
aware, to a certain extent, of the value of
another day; but are you really aware
of what it is for?
It is for the evolving of your soul.
It is for the ability to be
in the 'here and now' with Me.
To be in the holy moment with Me.
So welcome the bright dawn. Welcome the new
moment. For no matter what has gone before,
the chance to be aware, to be awake, to be with Me
is now!

16 December

The year draws to a close, a year with
its lights and shadows.
All opposites have walked hand in hand.
As the new year approaches, there is time to
think about all that has happened.

Nothing is by chance; therefore ask,
what has been learnt, what has been gained,
what has been lost?

Whatever answer presents before you,
evaluate and decide on how to live – how to
reorganise your existence.
This time of year reveals many opportunities
for reflection and self-discovery.

17 December

Many will question. Many will demand answers. A voice in your ear may speak.

Take all, as from those who would shelter you under their wings. From those who would shield you and hold you gently; from those who would protect you from your very self.

An answer is but a blink away, from the brilliantly lit path upon which you could be travelling.
Take heed, for when an answer comes in any form, it is your guidance towards the life that you should be living – to do the work that you came here to do.

18 December

Limitless is My Love for you.
Boundless and inexhaustible is the
source which you can access.

Know that you can call upon this
at any time. There is no early closing,
or late opening, on this storehouse.

Yet so many ignore, or even refuse
to become aware. Oh, how lives could change
for the better, if even one thought
were directed towards Me!

My power, My Love, My energy and
purpose will not be denied. For it is the
Divine Plan that all will come to know.

19 December

Let Me take your hand and guide
you to a world as yet unknown...

the world that lies around you!

The world where all that you would have
can be yours, by pure thought
alone. Let Me take all that you are,
and transform it into all that you
can be!

Creation awaits your call;
your direction lies with Me!

20 December

A step nearer to Me each time you
consciously stop and call Me.

A step nearer to the beautiful Light
that is now all around you.

You have called upon the highest, and
have been heard.

An answer is on its way, for the good
of all.

Seek not to justify any behaviour
that is not of truth and Love. For that will
only serve to endorse and encourage
ignorance. Seek only the truth,
which your heart knows is your guiding light,
and must be followed.

21 December

There can be no doubt as to the source of wisdom. There can be no doubt that all received is given in Love only, and totally free from contamination.

There can be no doubt that there is more to learn. More of which to become aware than anyone could imagine.

There is One who has lived in your heart for all time; One who knows you better than you know yourself.
One who is Mother/Father both, and is the gentle voice that calls.

22 December

Wake up now, for this is your call.

This is your time, to come into another place. And yet, it is the same place that you have always been.

Wake up now, and listen to what is being imparted. Your soul must be set free!
It can take imprisonment no longer.

To know Me is to be free.

23 December

All must follow their hearts, for to do otherwise would create unbearable sorrow. To search for the path is a right... for all.

And doing so will return you to the One who knows you. Come back to the source of all truth. Let none be misled!

Let none be ensnared into false ways of being.

24 December

Grieve not overlong for what is passed,
For it cannot and will never be as it was.

All is but an illusion.
So grow more secure, with the only reality.
Grow, until you are able to withstand all.
For you fight a formidable foe; you stand
alone against ignorance.

But your efforts are not in vain: the One
who sees and knows your struggles
will wipe away every tear.

Be strong in My name, and remember –
it is a holy time.

25 December

Come to My table, clothed not in garments of falsehood, pride or ego, but in garments of the purest white.

Leave your sandals at the door, for long and dusty has been your journey. Rest now in the company of friends.

Come with Love in your heart; for only those will partake of the holy meal.

And there at the table, sit by My side, for we will gather together and share all that we have at this time.

26 December

Do you not see that all is by design? All that you do is governed. Therefore, keep faith with Me, for we walk together.

Know that one may help another. For there will be times when one is stronger and will support, until life energy flows back into body, mind and heart.

Resolve is renewed; vigour is revitalised.

27 December

I will find a home in the humble heart.
For only such as these will receive Me,
for they are open to My words.

When the way forward seems unclear
and blocked; there is no other alternative
but to practice stillness of mind and body,
and in doing so, all will become clear again.

Let your soul soar with joy unbounded.
For you have been given a rare and
wondrous gift – a gift that is available to all,
who would come into silence and meet Me.

28 December

Let sorrow be at an end now. Rest your
head upon My shoulder.

There are so many who Love you, and
only that will manifest in your life from
now on!

Bless all experiences, even if, at the time,
you judge them bad;
for they lead you to Me.

29 December

Is there one amongst the crowd
who would risk all for Me? Is there one
on whom I could depend? Could it be you?

If I called at your house tomorrow and
said, 'Will you live your life for Me?'
what would be your answer?

I do not ask every person. I know who I
want on My side; not all come close
to the requirements.

I choose carefully when I ask,
'Is there one here?'

30 December

Tiptoe silently towards the door.
A gentle tap is all that is necessary.
I await the sound, and will open it
to greet you. We smile as we recognise
each other.

Old friends, reunited in an embrace
of homecoming. You are welcomed in,
and once there, all shadows fall away.

All heaviness departs.
For in the approaching, the knocking,
the opening, all becomes known.

31 December

Take the hand that I offer you,
and step over the threshold.

Let your eyes feast upon another vision —
an abundant world of Love.
This is yours for the asking; yours for
the living.

This is the gift of which I speak:
My Love in your soul, to share and let
others see the Light, so that they might
come to know Me.

Thank you.

www.ingramcontent.com/pod-product-compliance
Lightning Source LLC
Chambersburg PA
CBHW022203090526
44583CB00012BA/294